AF408365

PACKING UP

PACKING UP

On Hearing God, Healing and Purpose

JAN AND AL CHERBONNEAU

Four Marks Publishing

Contents

Copyright © 2023 by Jan and Al Cherbonneau

All rights reserved. No part of this book may be reproduced in any manner whatsoever without written permission except in the case of brief quotations embodied in critical articles and reviews.

First Printing, 2023

The cover artwork is the painting "Tree of Life #1" by Mark Betson, used by permission

The bible citations in this work are taken from either the New International Version (NIV) or the New American Bible, Saint Joseph Edition (NAB) with the source cited in each quote.
The Holy Bible, New International Version, Copyright © 1973, 1978, 1984 by International Bible Society
The Saint Joseph Edition of The New American Bible, Copyright © 1970, 1986, 1991 by Catholic Book Publishing Co., New York

Looking back, we give great thanks to our family, our churches, and our friends, for their love, guidance, and encouragement in the use of our gifts.

Looking forward, we give thanks for all who may read this work and find it a blessing in some way.

Looking beyond time, we give inexpressible thanks to the Holy Trinity, Father, Son, and Holy Spirit, as well as for the ongoing prayers of the Blessed Virgin Mary and the Communion of Saints.

I

Introduction

In 1992, some months after my husband, Allen and I arrived in Ambridge, Pennsylvania to attend seminary, I felt a strong leading from the Lord to write about the remarkable physical, emotional, and spiritual journey that had taken us there. That task, and that assignment, would prove to be enormously challenging, as it involved the interweaving of several rich and complex strands. The first of these strands centered on how we began the process of learning to hear and follow the Lord. The second strand involved my miraculous deliverance from ovarian cancer, while the third described my, and our, surrounding and subsequent journeys of emotional healing. But most importantly, as we walked the path of obedience, we were to discover that each of these strands had been deliberately and inextricably entwined with a fourth strand--that of our initial stages of discernment of call, of purpose, and of life direction.

As I drew near to the conclusion of that early manuscript, I agonized over an appropriate ending point for the story. When we prayed for clarity, however, Allen instead thought he received a most enigmatic word from the Lord: *"Maybe it is two books."* At the time, all I could assume was that the Lord perhaps wanted me to write a sequel, suggesting that I should begin a second book at the point where I had left off with the first, but I was uncertain even about that. Try as I might to ponder this cryptic word, it did nothing but puzzle and frustrate me, for I wanted a simple answer to what I thought was a relatively simple question, and I wanted it *then*. That did not happen and, after awhile, I decided to put my efforts aside until the Lord chose to show me more clearly what He wished me to do.

It would be three years later, after our arrival in Alabama in 1996, that we received a further word on the matter. The Lord now seemed to be saying that my first work needed to be more overtly and intentionally focused on the subject of hearing God. All well and good, I reasoned, but some initial attempts in that direction still left me wondering just what I was supposed to do, and how I was to do it.

Four more years passed, and, in October of 2000, we returned from Russia with our three adopted siblings. Again, God called me to write and I did so, telling the amazing story of how we came to have our children. I passed the finished story on to a friend who had some editorial experience, and she suggested that I incorporate the adoption story into a book on hearing God. Things were now beginning to come full circle. Indeed, as I began that project, some nine years after writing my original manuscript, I realized that I could use sizable segments of my earlier work. Ultimately, that book became Two Eggs, Three Yolks: Learning To Hear and Follow God. Part I explained how we came to begin the hearing process, Part II was a detailed instruction manual, and Part III consisted of the adoption story itself, which served well as an extended and fascinating example of the process in action.

As it happens, I *did* continue to write, but our second book took a very different direction, as one might guess from its title: Every Spiritual Blessing: The Unusual Story of How We Came to the Catholic Church. More recently, we published our third book, The Parable of Snickers and Other Reflections: Eternity Hidden in the Ordinary, and we have recently published a rewrite of our first book, now titled Learning to Hear and Follow God, a Manual with Illustrations. Now, in this fifth and present work, we are returning to the "second" book contained in our original manuscript: a study of healing and purpose in the context of hearing God using, amidst other things, my own remarkable story of physical and emotional healing. I remain astonished as I think back to the Lord's puzzling hint from so long ago, for I now see that my first effort had indeed been "two books!" I have also learned, I might add, that when the Lord says *"Maybe..."* regarding an issue, there is usually a large wink involved, since He wisely chooses to leave it to us to discover and work through the implications of His words, rather than simply spelling things out for us.

As I have worked on this book, I have often praised the Lord that, painful and difficult as it had been at the time--both from a literary and an emotional standpoint, I had persisted through that earliest writing. It has saved me enormous time, but, far more importantly, things that I would now no longer recall clearly enough, both in terms of details and of emotions, were recorded while they were fresh. Though that first work, as a single book, was shelved, the Lord had known what He was asking me to do at the time, and why. I include these details in the hopes that other writers may be encouraged. My advice in these circumstances is to journal, keep the journals (!), jot down initial thoughts, make outlines, keep the manuscripts, get some sage counsel, and continue praying for guidance. Thankfully, having done those things myself, I am now better equipped to embark on the task of relating and exploring the intimate connections between hearing God, healing, in its fullest and deepest sense, and the seeking, finding, and fulfilling of His ongoing purposes for us. Not surprisingly, it is in the scriptures themselves where we encounter this *shalom*--the all-encompassing term that makes of this endeavor a cohesive whole.

Shalom is a wondrously rich Hebrew word--indeed, one of the most important words in the theology of the Old Testament, and it also lies at the heart of everything this book is about. It is appropriate, then, to pause here and examine the word's many nuances. This word is most succinctly translated as "peace," and, in contemporary Hebrew parlance, it is the ordinary way to convey a greeting or a goodbye. But it has always been about vastly more than cordial well wishing or the simple *absence* of conflict. The word is alive with positive energy, with an exhortation to life-giving thought and activity. Indeed, its root, *shalem*, encompasses physical healing, wholeness, well-being, a sense of purpose, unity, restitution, payment of debts, bestowal of blessing, harmony, forgiveness, restored relationships, and an abiding peace flowing from peace with God and neighbor.

We believe that God is calling His people to hear His guidance, both in scripture and through daily prayer, regarding our mental, physical, emotional, and spiritual healing. But the journey doesn't stop there, for the wider call also draws us *outward*, to issues of relationship with God and with others--all in the context of our discernment of vocation and of life purpose. We are thus called to a responsibility before the Lord to be stewards, not only of our bodies, but of our general well-being (our *shalom*) and, ultimately, of our *very* being. That is both a high calling and a great responsibility, but it is also an endeavor that is filled with true adventure and joy.

Again, that process is rooted and grounded, not only in scripture, but also in the ongoing conversation between the Good Shepherd and His sheep. And so, on one occasion, Allen thought he heard the Lord say this about the meaning of *shalom* with regard to His objectives concerning our greater healing:

> *Healing is indeed a concept that many misunderstand. I am not looking to simply repair what is broken or out of place, but I am looking to grow 'shalom,' and sometimes illness can be a fertile ground for 'shalom.' I have a bigger goal in mind than just physical fitness or mental health, as good as those things might be. I am about an adventure that is tied into the whole of every self and the whole of My creation. There is a depth to all of this that can be elusive in the midst of the daily struggles with cares and upsets and pains and trouble, but it is there nonetheless, and it is tied into the highest purpose that I have for each life. You have been learning much, and you have had some distress with this process, but it is a*

*journey that is worth taking, and it will continue to lead you
into new adventures.*

Healing, then, is not about getting fixed so that we can get on with our own agendas. It is not simply about figuring out how to do a better (and less painful) job of getting better, and it is surely not about the spiritual manipulation of God, were that even possible. It is about joy, hope, *true* comfort, *real* peace, wholesome laughter, and the forming of lasting and meaningful relationships. It is about gaining an eternal perspective on the ultimate nature and purpose of suffering. Healing involves an unrelenting process of stretching, struggle, and pain--what might be called "holy *discomfort*." The spiritual healing involved in *shalom* is hard work--the hardest, really--for it is about the work of on-going self-examination and of forming honest relationships with God and with others, the means by which we are justified, sanctified, and glorified. This is the great adventure of life. If we are in Christ, healing becomes not only the heart of the journey but the journey of the heart, for this is His highest and deepest goal for us. When asked what the greatest commandment was, Jesus answered, "The first is this: 'Hear, O Israel! The Lord our God is Lord alone! You shall love the Lord your God with all your heart, with all your soul, with all your mind, and with all your strength.' The second is this: 'You shall love your neighbor as yourself.' There is no other commandment greater than these." (Mark 12: 29-31 NAB) It is not by accident that our words *salve* and *salvation* spring from the same linguistic roots, for, ultimately, if we not are found in Christ, true healing will haunt but forever elude us.

We struggle to understand why we do not see more physical, spiritual, or emotional healing, though the reasons are usually both far more simple and far more challenging than we wish to acknowledge. We bemoan what we see as our failures, we agonize over and adjust our techniques of praying, we regularly become angry with God, with others, and with ourselves, and sometimes, we just plain quit trying. However, the answers that elude us are both more and less obvious. Our greater healing, to the degree that we will grasp it this side of glory, is a function of hearing God in His scriptures, in His Church, and in our hearts, and then being in line with His sovereign will for our lives. We want to overly spiritualize the matter of faith, making of it a noble, if somewhat ethereal virtue, whereas God always means faith to be a vigorously active pursuit of, and even a wrestling with, His will. The ability to hear God is not only a gift and a privilege, but it is also an ongoing challenge and responsibility. While God is always gracious and merciful, He also expects and, in fact, commands us to actively participate with Him in the transforming pursuit of our own well-being--our *shalom*. This is a critical part of what it means to work out our *salvation*--our ultimate healing--with fear and trembling. (Philippians 2:12).

We humans often have a rather simplistic and one-dimensional view of healing. We think it means recovering from the chicken pox, mending from a broken arm, having successful surgery, or receiving and applying some good counseling. Those things are all good and desirable, but, as the above words from the Lord underscore, it is His highest will, His greatest desire, that we live in and move toward *shalom* which, if we have been faithful, will be complete wholeness and well-being finally realized in the age to come. That process can only be engaged through wrestling and resting; seeking and abiding; straining forward and quietly listening, all of which come only through the continual hearing process. *Shalom* is about the profound connection between doing and being. As the Lord reminds us, "My sheep hear my voice; I know them, and they follow me." (John 10: 27 NAB)

Now that we have begun to explain what this book is about, we will take a moment to say what it is *not*. First, this book will be neither comprehensive nor exhaustive in scope, both for our sake and for the reader's--and, of course, that would be utterly impossible anyway, since the subject would fill many libraries. Second, it will not be our task to attempt to engage in an examination of the intimate relationship between hearing, healing, and purpose in the scriptures themselves, though that is a fascinating and worthy theme. Third, since the focus *is* on our personal experience, we have also set aside all corporate, church, world, and national issues involving healing and purpose-- topics that would fill many more libraries. Despite all of this, we could scarcely begin to deal with the wealth of material from *our own* experience. So, we are, on the Lord's advice, restricting our narrative content to that which relates how our healing journey moved forward. In other words, we are using our story, but not simply retelling our story. Story is the *vehicle*, the lens through which the reader will get a glimpse into what it looked like to invite the Holy Spirit to be our Guide on the journey to healing, calling, and destiny. Our hope is that, our story, while personal, will speak to the *commonality* of human experience and the ultimate questions of "Who am I?", "Where am I going?", "What is my purpose?", and "What is the ultimate purpose of life, both here and in eternity?"

Further, we have also chosen not to include examples from the hundreds of instances in which the Lord gave us words regarding the *physical* health concerns that came up in the course of our daily lives during this time. While general principles do apply, these situations were personal, and the Lord's remedies were prescriptive *to us*. We might add, though, that in those situations, He indeed has always proven Himself to be the Great Physician. After all, He alone knows what is going on in every cell of our bodies at every moment, and He alone discerns our hearts and our inmost thoughts. The exceptions here are found in my two stories of healing found in Section Two of this book, since they are integral parts of those stories.

Again, this shall not be another book amidst many on the *general* subjects of physical healing, inner healing, or the healing ministry, from a Christian perspective. Neither is it an *analytical* study of the complex interconnections between the physical, mental, and spiritual dimensions of our wellbeing. Those crucial connections will be readily and abundantly apparent in the stories we relate. Rather, this work is born of our conviction that healing and hearing the Lord are inextricably bound together by the cords of the Lord's temporal and eternal *purposes* for us, and that will be our overarching theme, as underscored and illuminated by this portion of our own journey. Indeed, when Allen and

I sought the Lord about the scope and focus of this book, He further refined the parameters for us in this way:

> *You can only write effectively about what you have experienced with Me. There are surely some miraculous healings that I do for My own purposes at particular times. However, I have not done that with you. I have used words of guidance and specific directions to work physical and emotional healing. You don't even really know the extent of the healing, since you don't know what might have happened without your obedience in a number of areas. Your obedience has certainly not been perfect, but it has done more than you understand. I do not work in the same way in every life, for My intent is to bring people into the fullest use of their gifts and their interests. You don't need to write a textbook on every type of healing, but you can use the range of your own experiences as parameters for your work.*

And so, in obedience to God's call, we will begin by recounting, in some detail, my two stories of healing, and of my, and our, journeys toward physical and emotional healing in the context of calling. We will also relate our journey from home to seminary and far beyond--a journey in which we both found the healing and the joy that come from the discovery and pursuit of our true life purposes.

As we began this challenging assignment, we sought the Lord further for a clear sense of focus and direction. Not surprisingly, Allen thought he heard Him say:

> *Hearing Me is the central element, the theme that guides to life-changing decisions, and finding My purpose is the ultimate goal. Your focus is on telling the story of how I have led you to healing through a process of following My guidance. It is the flow of what I did as a whole because you were willing*

*to listen. You want to draw the readers into your journey to
help them desire their own journey.*

On another occasion, as we inquired regarding the *method* with
which to proceed, the Lord gave these instructions:

> *Choose particular events and 'journeys' that show the hearing
> process so that there is a continuous story. Your healing and
> the journey to Ambridge are the core, though other things
> will fit in well. This is a way to relive, rejoice in, and recount
> your story to help others.*

As has been the case with each of our books, the themes, the purpose, and the take-away for the reader have consistently come through
this medium of *story*. As primary writer (Jan) of the text, storytelling is
both who I am and what I do. Thus, when I queried the Lord as to why
the context of *this* book should also be our own story, He offered both
a common sense reminder and an exhortation: *"Indeed, you cannot avoid
telling your story, but it must relate to those who need the lessons."* Herein lay
the directive, as well as the great challenge, for the work would involve
sorting through massive amounts of journal material in order to distill
what would be most helpful to the reader. As I further asked the Lord
for clarity of focus for this project, Allen thought he heard Him say:

> *The process of being willing to take the steps to hearing Me is
> in itself part of the journey of healing. Hearing My guidance is
> bound to your breaking free from the spiritual, psychological,
> and even physical chains that bind you. Thus, in some sense,
> the journey to hearing parallels the journey to healing.*

This book, then, is all about healing in the context of hearing God
and seeking and living out His purposes.

As one might by now expect, Allen and I continued to seek the Lord for direction, and He gave us these crucial and challenging words regarding the spiritual roots of all illness and the foundations of real healing:

There are, of course, different levels of healing, from that at a personal level, to that at the level of a small group, to that which involves large numbers of people--even a nation. I desire all of those levels of healing to occur, but they are obviously very different in some ways. The similarity is that the root cause is sin, though the sin may not be that of the individual, or even of the present larger group. Sin always has consequences that play out, even when repentance removes the condemnation. Sin is like kudzu: once the seed is planted, it is very, very difficult to remove. The bad news is that sin is a human condition, but the good news is that I AM a Savior; that is, for those who trust Me, there are no eternal effects. Even if a human being, other than Me, led a sinless life, there are still the effects of all of the other sin in the world, some of which will have an effect upon that one. However, those who will accept My guidance and be obedient will find that My path is the best protection against the raging storm of sin. My people can choose to walk the best way, if they will listen, or they can choose to battle against the sin without My guidance, though they always have My help if they will take it. Surely, My scriptures are a general map that will keep many under some protection, but they cannot know how to avoid the particular storms of sin in their lives without My specific guidance. Healing is, in its fullest sense, something that will not be accomplished until I return, but it is something that can come, in part, through listening and obedience, both for individuals and for those groups willing to hear. None of this is easy, but I provide blessing and encouragement for those who are willing to walk on the edge, trusting Me rather than the wisdom of the world. The irony is that it only seems like the edge, for it is the safest place in the world.

And again,

You have learned that hearing Me is one essential component of the fulfilled life of a Christian. There can be no real healing without confronting the things that I bring into the light. All sickness and death has some sort of a spiritual root, though it is not all directly related to the suffering individual. However, there is no complete innocence in any of this, for all have sinned and fall short of My glory. I would that all know the grace and the healing that is possible through being attentive to My voice--first in the scriptures, and then in answer to prayer: in conversation, if you will. I place scripture first because someone who will not seek Me in scripture will not seek Me for wisdom and guidance. Even if they did, they would not have the understanding to judge My voice without scripture. Therefore, what you have been urged to write is exceedingly necessary, and it is difficult because it is at the core of My work, and, in the end, it involves not only individuals, but relationships, families, communities, nations, and the strife of the whole creation. You cannot write about all of that, but you can write about what you know, and that is all I ever ask.

Hopefully, then, this work will demonstrate how this process of hearing, of healing, and of discernment of call was lived out, as we took what we were so wisely and graciously handed, prayed to discern God's direction, step by step, and followed to the best of our ability. We think it's a pretty good story, and we trust you will, too!

2

Two Stories of Healing

Before I begin these healing narratives, I must pause here to deal with an issue that came up as I first began to read over and edit these stories, a number of years after they were initially written. As I pored over the text of what I had penned those years ago, it did not take me long to realize, with some dismay, that I was now at a different place in my thinking--something, I might add, that is largely inevitable. Thus, I was questioning not only the dogmatism with which I now saw myself as having interpreted the words, dreams, and visions but, further, some of the very applications I had chosen to assign to those things. So, what was I to do? The only option seemed to be to eliminate all commentary and leave the interpretation to the reader, but I couldn't see how that would allow the narrative to hang together. Allen and I brought the dilemma to the Lord, and we offer here what seemed to be His response:

> *You can obviously not be dogmatic about interpretation, but you can say that you understood My words in a particular way at that time, which led you to take the subsequent actions. You are not capable of understanding any word outside of the bounds of your own histories, experiences, and*

awareness; therefore, all of your response to Me will be bounded by those conditions. That is not a bad thing, for it is the human condition, but My words are able to be seen in a number of ways—though never contradictory. Therefore, you are free to write with the understanding that you interpreted in a particular way because of your situation, and I knew that you would interpret that way when you got the word. It is the truth, but it is not the whole truth, so your writing should reflect that understanding. You are aware that even receiving words from Me is a process that involves hearing through the wall of your own sin, so you "hear through a wall 'darkly,'" so to speak. You are seeking Me in a diligent and regular way, so you are protected from gross error by continually seeking understanding. That does not mean that your hearing is perfect, but it is adequate to the things to which you are called, and adequate to the issues of hearing My voice for guidance in a variety of ways. As you are writing the book, you can do no other but interpret, but you only must qualify that these interpretations are not absolute or complete understandings. My goal is that you be on a journey to shalom.

I submit this word for several reasons. First, I trust that it will be of good help to the reader in his or her own walk, as it speaks much to the process of interpreting, and interpreting over time. Second, the word clearly underscores once more the importance of hearing God in any undertaking, here most particularly with regard to writing about experiences from a spiritual perspective. In this case, God's wisdom gave peace and permission, boundaries and freedom, cutting through the confusion with which we had been plagued. Third, the word helps keep us spiritually tuned-in to God's work in our lives. And last, it is a reminder that my interpretations, where indicated, reflect who I was in my own sanctification process at the time. Where I have subsequently been given new insights, I will include them.

I will now describe in some detail two healing events from my own history. As I recount these experiences, I encourage the reader to be looking for the connections between hearing God and healing. It will become evident that, in one way or another, each of these elements was woven into the complex fabric of the Lord's work in me, and, by extension, in both of us. My prayer is that by sharing my struggle to become both physically well and emotionally free, I may perhaps spare others some pain by providing some useful insights into their own situations. At the same time, however, I do bear in mind these words, more profoundly theological than I suspect they were meant it to be, printed on a bottle of Jamaican hot sauce in my refrigerator: "Pain is good." My stories of healing and deliverance are an integral and pivotal part of our larger journey and call, as they ultimately are for all who choose to hear, follow, and obey.

3

Setting the Background

My own journey of healing and deliverance had its beginnings in the pain of family co-dependency and emotional illness. I am an only child and, while my parents were, in most respects, tremendously loving and supportive, there had also been dangerous undercurrents present from my earliest childhood. As I have written elsewhere, my mother was brilliant, multi-talented, and often witty and charming, but she was also obsessively controlling and narcissistic, as well as, at times, physically, verbally, and emotionally abusive. My father, on the other hand, was overly passive, coping with my mother's behavior through a pattern of avoidance and denial. And, as they each grew older, those patterns not only solidified but intensified. The unfortunate mixture was a disaster in the making, and I was inevitably a victim. It was only when I began to be able to hear the Lord that I could see my situation more objectively, and thus start the process of choosing not to be victimized but, most importantly, to forgive.

I realized, in retrospect that, due to a combination of fear and misguided love, not to mention guilt, I had never accomplished the normal process of developing an adult relationship with my parents, particularly my mother. I had failed to establish appropriate spatial and emotional boundaries, and, indeed, I scarcely knew what those were. What's more, as she grew older, my mother's more difficult traits became the dominant ones until she became a rage-filled and abusive caricature of her formal self. Consequently, I began to dread each visit home, with its inevitable verbal assaults and irrationality. Meanwhile, my father's only response was further denial and withdrawal. Unfortunately, rather than distancing myself, I, as well as Allen, allowed ourselves to be drawn further and further into the craziness, opting to spend every Sunday with them under the delusion that we could somehow make things better by our presence. In the midst of it all, I also felt that I was somehow partly to blame for the dysfunction! On occasion, we did opt to stay away, but the simplest phone conversations were also painful, for even the more pleasant ones always left me feeling that I'd lost some elusive and intangible battle. Sadly, the problem didn't cease when we left, for the aftermath of our visits and phone calls was often a bout of misplaced rage directed at my husband or at some totally unrelated situation in my life--what psychologists call "kick the cat" syndrome. It would have been funny, if it hadn't been so awful, and yet I persisted.

However, the Lord was not pleased with my misguided devotion and began, quietly at first, and then more frequently and forcefully, to make it known that He wished me free and, in fact, would not rest until I *was* free. Left to my *own* devices, however, I may never have taken the necessary steps toward separation and healing, since I could not recognize the problem for what it was. Being an only child only served to exacerbate the situation. The amazing thing, consequently, was that in the process of *healing*, God allowed, in His infinite wisdom, two experiences of *illness*--a divine twist that is often part of the way He chooses to work. Thus, it was He Himself who initiated the healing process, using scripture, words, dreams, visions, and the ministrations of the Body of Christ, the Church, to bring me towards that wholeness of person He desires for all of us. Those experiences I will now describe, although much has been omitted, for the sake of the flow of the narratives.

The admonitions from the Lord concerning my unhealthy attachment to my parents had no doubt begun three or four years before when I suffered through a series of strange viral infections. In hindsight

I can see that my body was trying to tell me that I was exhausted, both physically and emotionally. It is the very nature of bondage to blind us to the truth--and thus, failing to see these illnesses as caution signs, I continued in a downward spiral of mental despair and physical debilitation. However, when the Lord has warned us repeatedly, and we have failed to heed, He then begins to work through circumstances--something I was about to experience first-hand! Looking back, it is apparent that the Lord was beginning to prepare Allen and me to distance ourselves--not only emotionally, but physically, as well. By His grace, and His design, the distancing would, in turn, be for the further purpose of training for the call that He had upon our lives. The move would also provide both a place and a space of time in which to find healing, community, and calling.

4

A Trip to the Dermatologist

Though the Lord had already been at work to produce the necessary change in us, I believe that His warnings, and in turn His healing, began in earnest in July of 1991. It started this way. One night, as I prayed about my father, Allen received this verse regarding Abraham and his nephew Lot: "so that the land could not support them if they stayed together; their possessions were so great that they could not dwell together." (Genesis 13:6 NAB)

The general application of the verse to our own situation was clear enough, in that it was about two relatives who, to avoid contention, were being called to separate themselves for the good of them both. Needless to say, however, we, as yet, had no idea as to what form that separation might take. Neither, like Abraham and Lot, could we discern how that separation would ultimately play out in the service of God's greater purposes. But the Lord was already on the move, and, though we could not as yet recognize it, our time of departure was evidently nearing. In preparation, however, I would first be required to make two unusual stops.

The first was to the dermatologist's office, where I was about to participate in a dress rehearsal for the larger drama that was soon to unfold.

For several months, I had had a nagging concern about a blackish mole on my left ankle and two on my back. By late July, this anxiety had increased sharply, and the moles were a constant source of worry. However, each time the anxiety arose, I would push down the rising sense that there might be a problem. In fact, I managed with some success to convince myself that the danger was all in my head--but the Lord knew differently.

One hot afternoon, I lay on the couch reading my new NIV Study Bible. I had just closed it, and was reaching to set it back on the coffee table, when I heard a very direct message, best described as a voice inside my head that I knew was not my own. It said, *"Read Leviticus 13:2."* My first inclination was to ignore the voice. After all, it is natural for us to think that we are merely hearing the interior musing of our own minds. But the urging was too clear, and too firm, and so I chose to obey. I opened the Bible again to the verse and read this: "When anyone has a swelling or a rash or a bright spot on his skin that may become an infectious skin disease, he must be brought to Aaron the priest or to one of his sons who is a priest." (Leviticus 13:2 NIV)

I was stunned, for I knew that, placed in a contemporary context, the Lord was telling me to present myself to a doctor for examination. Shaken, but determined to be obedient, I immediately grabbed my purse, jumped in the car, and drove to the dermatologist's office in the next town with the hope that he could see me immediately. Instead, I had nearly a month to wait.

However, as the date for the examination loomed closer, I began to come face to face with several hidden, but massive fear issues in my life, for I was terrified out of all proportion to the precautionary nature of the warning and the exam. Medical fears naturally seemed to be at the forefront: a terror of pain, of needles, of doctors, of hospitals, of the unknown, of losing control. Even worse, if I had a melanoma, was I going to die? I have since come to see that these were only the presenting issues signaling a host of deeper ones reaching back to my childhood. While rereading our journals, I had found the description of an intriguing vision that suddenly gave me some insights. The image consisted of a smoothly polished half-oval shaped piece of wood, with a slot cut diagonally into one side. Wood, I knew, symbolized humanity and the human body, and thus the piece might somehow have represented me, but what of the odd cut? Though I had come across the record of this image a few times before, I was suddenly quite sure in my spirit that the slot represented the somewhat diagonal scar on my abdomen from my appendectomy at the age of eleven. I had become violently ill shortly after midnight one night, and was rushed to the hospital and operated on just moments before my appendix, according to the surgeon, would have ruptured. I was so horribly sick that I remember weakly asking my parents from the backseat of the car if I was going to die. I had a good and speedy recovery, and the memory of that trauma has faded, but the Lord, it seemed, was indicating to me that the experience had left some lasting imprints.

An experience I had at the age of fourteen didn't help either. I had to have an overnight dental surgery, and the nurse who came in to insert my IV told me to inform her (!) when the IV fluid was running out. Well, I fell sound asleep, only to be awakened during the night by a terrible ache in that arm. When I looked up at the IV bag, not only was it empty, but it was half full of my own blood! I buzzed for the nurse, who, rather than apologizing or commiserating, proceeded to give her young charge a sharp scolding for falling asleep and not following her instructions! But the fun wasn't over yet, for two days later, I developed an awful infection in the roof of my mouth and for four days, even taking a sip of water was excruciatingly painful. By the time I had had some other minor surgeries, I was terrified at the thought of all things medical.

Not every kid who goes through these sorts of experiences has such a reaction later in life, so what, I wondered, was the real nature of my problem? Was it simply the memory of the frightening medical procedures? Of course, fear of pain and a fear of the unknown are common to the human condition, and they are all the more heightened in children. Indeed, as I write this, I am reminded of a comical little scenario Allen and I had witnessed while out for a walk one evening.

Ahead of us on the sidewalk were a mother and her four-year-old daughter, who was happily riding her tricycle. We strolled up behind them just in time to hear the mother say carefully, "Now, tomorrow you are going to the doctor." The child glanced up suspiciously, shot back "*I don't have a boo-boo!*" and peddled furiously away, while her mother's receding voice added faintly from behind, "You need to have your ears and tummy checked."

Yet I wondered, too, if my terror was related to something even more deeply rooted. I recalled that in the first hours after my appendectomy, and while in great pain, I had lain awake in the semi-darkness, anxiously waiting for my parents to come into the room, and frantically wondering where they were. After what seemed like an eternity, I cried out in fear and distress, "Where's my Mommy and Daddy?" At this, the mother seated next to her child in the other bed offered that it was the middle of the night, and that my parents had gone home for a while, and would be back in the morning. I was somewhat calmed, but also distressed that they had left me. Why was the other child's mother there for him while mine had gone home? And was the fear of abandonment now part of the unhealed pain? I also recalled that, while under the anesthesia, I had had a sense of being in a long, dark tunnel through which I was being tightly squeezed, while ahead of me was a brilliant yellow light toward which I was traveling. Current research suggests, perhaps, a near death experience; though I was never later told, nor may it have even been the case that I had nearly died. Nonetheless, I now wondered if I had somehow come face to face, for the first time in my young life, with the real possibility, and ultimate inevitability, of my own death. Abandonment and death--primal matters, these.

Later, as Allen and I sat down to pray about the upcoming doctor's visit regarding the moles, he recorded this:

> Jan and I are praying together about the moles on her
> back and ankle, asking that they be healed, and that her
> anxiety about them be lifted. As we prayed, I saw a hole
> with concentric circles around it, with a something like

a bombsight focused on it. As I watched, the hole shrank and disappeared. Then we prayed about possible harassing spirits, and I saw a square-shaped, white, ghostlike figure with two large eyes. I asked for a scripture, and thought I got 1 Cor. 2:13: "And we speak about them not with words taught by human wisdom, but with words taught by the Spirit, describing spiritual realities in spiritual terms." (NAB)

The image of the bombsight suggested that the Lord did intend to thoroughly remove the danger through surgery, figuratively blasting it away. Further, the ghostlike image implied that I was, in fact, being harassed by a spirit of fear and, more specifically perhaps, a fear of death. The verse also assured me that these messages were indeed from the Lord, and that they revealed spiritual truths. In light of the two images, I was reminded that visions are, indeed, striking examples of spiritual realities conveyed in spiritual terms.

I went into the doctor's appointment with much nervousness, but was hoping to hear, "These moles are nothing to worry about." Instead, as I pointed to the black spot on my ankle, the doctor bent over, peered intently at it, and then said, "Yep, I'd take *that* one off." This litany repeated three more times, for the exam had revealed yet another suspicious spot on my hip. "Well," I thought, "he'll just burn them off, won't he?" (I had had a wart removed that way a year before.) However, he immediately added, "There is a surgeon next door. I'll call and send you over." "*Surgeon?*" I wailed! These are just *moles*!" Suddenly, we were talking about needles and knives!

The following Monday, I found myself in the surgeon's office. "When do you want to schedule this?" he asked. I took the first available date, in order not to prolong the agony of waiting. "Fine," he said, "I'll make arrangements for the operating room." "*Operating room?*" I gasped. My heart pounded harder, and my anxiety shifted into high gear.

The night before the surgery, we prayed again, and Allen wrote: "Jan and I are praying together at home about her fear concerning the operation to remove the moles on her skin. As I prayed, I saw a white mountain, and then an object that looked like a pick ax, also white. Next I saw a line of light, as though forming a flight of steps."

In the scriptures, mountains can symbolize obstacles or difficulties, and I was clearly facing one, but they more often represent the Lord as our source of strength and righteousness, and this one was white. I was led to Psalm 36:6: "Your righteousness is like the mighty mountains, your justice like the great deep. O Lord, *you preserve both man and Beast.*" *(NIV, italics mine)*

The pick ax, like the bombsight, confirmed the removal of the moles through surgery. Of course, I'll take a scalpel over a pick ax any day, but again, we are dealing with imagery here. Further, the "ax" was likely white, not only because surgical instruments must be sterile, and because it was all ultimately in the Lord's hands, but also because its use would result in purity--cleanness at the site of each lesion and thus, an assurance that all would be well. This message of purity was reflected and expanded in the scripture verse which was given next: "Since we have these promises, dear friends, *let us purify ourselves from everything that contaminates body and spirit, perfecting holiness out of reverence for God.*" 2 Cor. 7: 1 (NIV, italics mine)

It began to be evident that there was more going on here than the simple removal of some moles. Not only was the body in need of purification, but the spirit, as well. The Lord, as always, was after the healing of the whole person. Once again, shalom and holiness were the goals, and this, I believe, was also the message of the flight of steps made of light. By enduring this experience, I would become stronger, climbing a few more challenging steps on the stairway of growth, sanctification, and trust. Of course, God does not test us to see how we will respond: He knows, and His tests are not intended to make us fail. Rather, His testing is given to teach us that we can not only survive, but also increase in spiritual strength, maturity, and wisdom.

But I sensed that the symbolism went still deeper. Ephesians 5:27 tells us that it was the purpose of Christ's death to: "...present her to himself as a radiant church, *without stain or wrinkle or any other blemish, but holy and blameless.*" (NIV, italics mine) Here, then, is the underlying purpose of *all* sanctification: Christ, as the Bridegroom, ever drawing the Church, His Bride, toward deeper holiness in preparation for the wedding at His Second Coming. The message is *never* simply for or about ourselves.

The other scripture given would soon prove to be amazingly pertinent. Romans 3:1-4a reads: "What advantage, then, is there in being a Jew, or what value is there in circumcision? Much in every way! First of all, they have been entrusted with the very words of God. What if some did not have faith? Will their lack of faith nullify God's faithfulness? Not at all! (NIV)

What was I to make of this? I had already noted that my surgeon's name most likely indicated a Jewish heritage. Was I being called to take this opportunity to witness to him about the Messiah? Paul's text reminded me that the Jews had received great blessings from God, and that in the wider context of salvation history, their situation and their circumstances are also unique. Nonetheless, back at home, as I prayed for my doctor, I felt both hope and concern. But now, many years later, I find myself in another sort of joyous place, space, and time, for as I have noted earlier, we have undergone our own conversion, this one to the Catholic Church. There, we have been blessed and enriched by Jewish convert Roy Schoeman's exegesis of Romans 11, unpacked as only a Jew could do it, and indeed as only Roy could do it. I can honestly say that that was the first time I had ever really understood Paul's discourse regarding the role of the Jews, vis-a-vis the Gentiles, in salvation history. Now, anxiety and concern have been replaced with hope and reassurance regarding God's plan, God's timing, and the unfolding of His purposes.

The morning of the surgery found me pacing the hospital corridor, knees weak and palms sweating. I was ushered into the operating room, and when the doctor walked in, he found me sitting on the operating table, my wobbly legs dangling over the edge. I said, "I think I'm going to throw up." It wasn't just a turn of phrase. He replied, "If you only knew what a big nothing this was, you would laugh at yourself. You should see the *really serious* surgical situations I've had to deal with this week." I knew he was right. What's more, I had expected to see him clad head to toe in green surgical garb and mask, or at least in a white lab coat. Instead, he was wearing a plaid sports shirt and chinos.

The procedure was to take an hour. As I lay on the table while the doctor numbed each site, then cut and sewed, I gradually found that the experience was not so bad after all. It was indeed a "big nothing." As my terror began to subside, we began to converse. First, I shared the story of Leviticus 13:2, and how I had come to be on that table. This prompted him to share the story of his son's circumcision. We also traded stories of our experiences in Israel, and we had a good time conversing.

When the surgery was over, he gave me a prescription for a strong painkiller, adding, "You will probably need these when the anesthesia wears off in three or four hours." I filled the prescription, went home, and got into bed, there to await the worst. But now, with the trauma behind me, I could truly grasp and accept what the Lord had promised: deliverance. Satan's plans to harm me had been defeated. I lay there thanking and praising the Lord for His goodness.

After an hour or two, when no pain had begun, I got up, dressed, and went grocery shopping. That evening I went to Bible study at church. Still I felt no pain. In fact, I never had even the faintest twinge of pain or discomfort. The pills remained unopened in the medicine cabinet for years. While the range of discomfort experienced after this type of surgery can certainly vary from person to person, it is not likely that four inch-long incisions should have caused absolutely no sensation of discomfort. It is my conjecture that perhaps God allowed this blessing because I had been so prompt in my obedience, despite my fear.

When I went back to the doctor's office a week later to have the stitches removed, the biopsies were all negative. However, the cells in each of the four moles had been different, and all four were of types known to later become malignant, and quickly so. One mole, the doctor said, had been especially dangerous.

As the doctor left the room, he glanced back, his hand on the doorknob, and grinned. "Keep on reading the Good Book," he said. I was pleased that my witness had clearly made some impact, but I also wondered if I could not have presented the Gospel more explicitly.

Looking back, I am amazed at the multiplicity of works that the Lord had accomplished through this one incident:

1. On the strictly physical level, He had graciously warned me of danger, and then healed and delivered me.

2. He showed me symbolically that I was also in need of further sanctification, meaning that there were still issues of sin, rebellion, and lack of forgiveness in my life with which I needed to deal.

3. Further still, He revealed that He was zealous to likewise purify His bride, the Church, in preparation for His return.

4. I saw that I was being asked to witness to the Gospel, even, or perhaps especially, in the context of pain, fear, discomfort, inconvenience, or expense. It wasn't merely about me. In fact, nothing really is, if we are listening. Others are always meant to benefit, to receive blessing.

5. I learned that I was being tested, in order that I might be strengthened in faith and trust.

6. I realized that I was being called to confront deep and hitherto hidden fears.

7. I was reminded of the reality that there is no growth without pain, and that the lessons learned are ultimately the point of it all.

8. In retrospect, I would understand that I had been rehearsing for a far more serious medical adventure, looming just around the corner.

In the meantime, our own dialogue with the Lord concerning His will for our lives continued and intensified. Indeed, over the next few months, His voice seemed to grow stronger and more urgent. Perhaps we were also learning, through both practice and exigency, to hear Him better. In reading back over our prayer journals from this period, I can readily recapture the tension that was building as we moved towards the coming crisis for which the small moles, it seemed, had been a preparation and a dress rehearsal.

5

Hystorectomy

"But what can I say?
He has spoken to me,
and He himself has done this.
I will walk humbly all my years..."
(King Hezekiah, Isaiah 38:15 NIV)

Though there had doubtless been many previous words from the Lord concerning this situation, I will choose as a beginning point for this narrative a day in early August of 1991. I had stopped to visit a friend, and a heated discussion arose as to what we each perceived to be the best directions for my future. On returning home, I was directed to Frances J. Roberts' devotional, Come Away My Beloved, and led to read page 28. The title of the page was "The Divine Commission," and it read in part as follows:

"My child, do not chafe at the bit. *It is I who have put it in thy mouth.* I would have led thee by Mine eye, but ye have been willful and stubborn. Ye question My direction because it is not the common way. But I would have thee take a path that is quite different from *the paths of thy friends,* and it is because I would bring thee into a place in Me and a ministry in which they have no part. Do not hesitate, and do not falter. Move in and do so quickly, for I say unto thee, *the hour is late,* and there is great urgency because of the swiftness of the gathering darkness.... Even so it is coming to pass, that in this hour ye should be gripped with one consuming purpose--to find the place I have for thee. *I have deliberately put thorns in thy nest in order to drive thee forth. I understand thy reluctance, but I shall surely deal with thee until ye break out of thy bondage.* The enemy shall hinder thee in every way imaginable if ye give him any room to stand. Rebuke every detaining circumstance in My Name, and keep thyself covered by the blood. The preaching of the Gospel is still His will, and the salvation of souls is His chief concern. So also should it be thine, and nothing else should be permitted to take precedence over evangelism in thy life. Be diligent. *Confess thy lack, and repent of thy negligence.* Then shall I give thee a fresh anointing and a new commission. Behold, the hour is upon thee. Look not back. Go straight forward, nor allow any to detain thee or turn thee aside. My purposes can only be fulfilled as ye give Me your undivided loyalty." (italics mine)

The passage could not have been more pertinent to my own situation, but I also offer it here lest we presume that God, as I have already noted, would not allow pain and suffering, for His greater purposes and our greater healing.

After having begun, the Lord's messages now continued in a steady flow. One afternoon in September of 1991, while praying and meditating on the Lord and His will for me, I heard the word *"nascent."* I once again reached for my dictionary and was reminded that the word meant "beginning to exist or develop." Did this refer to the masses in my abdomen, as yet unknown to me, or to a new emotional and spiritual life beginning to grow within? Or was it the suppressed desire for children? Was the illness, the problem, of a psychosomatic nature? I suspect the word may have referred to all of these since, as noted, I have been repeatedly astounded by the Lord's masterful use of words and symbols. This made all the more fascinating the scripture that was given shortly afterwards: "Sing, O barren woman, you who never bore a child; burst into song, shout for joy, you who were never in labor; because more are the children of the desolate woman than of her who has a husband, says the Lord." (Isaiah 54:1 NIV)

Just as exiled and barren Israel was restored, so too would I be. I would have no natural offspring but, in due time, three adopted, as well as many more spiritual children, including thirteen foreign exchange students, dozens of Religious Education pupils--and now a beautiful little granddaughter, as well! But I'm getting ahead of myself.

October 24th of 1991 brought another reminder from the Lord, as well as a conditional promise. Allen and I had been contemplating a trip to Israel in March with a friend. As we prayed about the possibility of taking this tour, the Lord replied, *"Let me lead."* Then, directing Himself to me, He added, *"Remember your message from Come Away My Beloved."* I inwardly winced at these words, for I sensed that there would perhaps be a trip, but that it would be in the *Lord's* timing, following a period of divine discipline. He continued with the word *"Phoenix."* Our dictionary described the phoenix as "a mythical bird of great beauty, the only one of its kind, fabled to burn itself on a funeral pyre, and to rise from its ashes in the freshness of youth and live through another cycle of years." Here we saw an allusion to resurrection, but the word spoke more immediately of my own dying to self and rebirth to God's purposes. As with the word *"nascent,"* the Lord was speaking once again of *my own birthing* as a new creation in Him, followed by the promise of a life of service.

In this way, over a three-month period, the Lord had begun to fit together the pieces of His plan. I was in bondage, and I was to be "dealt with." God's loving correction would teach others, my healing would glorify God, and my own rebirth would bear much fruit. The Lord, we have noticed, persistently repeats His themes in different ways, until we get His message! Nonetheless, despite all that had already been revealed by Him, I didn't have a clue as to what lay immediately before me. I suppose I was like Jesus' disciples for, despite all His words to them concerning His resurrection, they could neither imagine nor comprehend what would need to happen first.

Meanwhile, if I was in a spiritual birthing process, I had felt only minor twinges, but full labor was about to begin. At the end of October, Betty Shepherd, an Australian woman with a teaching and healing ministry, came to our area to do a weekend-long mission. I had been bothered for some time with painful fibroid cysts in my breasts, and they had been particularly worrisome and uncomfortable just prior to and during Betty's time of ministry with us. By no coincidence, she devoted much of her teaching to the relationship between family dysfunction and illness. During a healing prayer service, Betty laid hands on me and, as she began to pray, I felt an urging from the Lord to simply give up control. On returning to my pew, I had a vision of Jesus coming along beside me, and taking my hand. We walked off into the distance side by side, I slightly behind, as though following His lead. "Walk after Me," He had so often said to His disciples. It was a command and an invitation. Glancing to my side, I noted with astonishment that I had been sitting next to a stained glass window depicting Miriam, sister of Moses, dancing on the shore of the Red Sea. In her upraised arm was a tambourine; in the background were the pyramids of Egypt. (See Exodus 15: 19-21) It was no coincidence that I had been sitting in that spot.

On leaving a later teaching session, I knelt at the chapel altar rail for a brief private prayer, and was astonished to hear the Lord say, *"Take up your tambourine, for you shall be delivered!"* Like Miriam, I would rejoice in my freedom from bondage, and would dance in victory as the waters closed over my largely internal enemies. What I could not understand at the time was that my deliverance from immediate physical danger would also usher in a lengthy wilderness period of further testing and refining. Indeed, at this point, I did not know of the danger at all.

In the meantime, the painful fibroid cysts in my breasts had worsened, and I again sought the Lord for healing. His cryptic comment was: *"A change of seasons."* No doubt He was referring to the hormonal changes going on at that particular time in my body, but I sensed that more was implied. Was I about to come into a new season in both my natural and my spiritual life? As I asked further about the pain, the Lord added, *"It's symbolic."* Many years later, I saw that the breast pain might well have been a physical reflection of the pain in my relationship with my mother, combined with the unrecognized longing for children of my own to nurture. After all, these two themes were profoundly interconnected. Some time later, I "stumbled upon" a confirmation of this in an article by a doctor concerning breast discomfort. Referring to the emotional message behind the physical symptoms, she wrote: "This is absolutely the first thing I look at. When I ask my patients, 'What's going on in your life around the issue of nurturing and being nurtured?' I often see tears. That's how closely linked breasts are to the emotions."

As we prayed about this, the Lord recommended exercise, most likely as a stress reducer and as a way to help regulate the estrogen in my system. He then went on to say, *"I am working more directly. The time is soon."* I understood Him to mean that He was dealing with me in a more overt way in order to accomplish His purposes in me more quickly. He added some further advice: *"Focus on others. Don't be anxious. The burdens are mine."* It was good advice then, and it is still good advice today, and not only for me, but for *all* those who seek healing. I could now see that my self-absorption with my own emotional pain was being physically manifested, and that I was being called to forget about myself and minister to others.

It was on the morning of December 4th, 1991 that I first noticed an odd and troubling hardness directly behind my navel. I had some concern, but I convinced myself that it was likely due to some extra exercise I had been doing. Since I already had my regular gynecological exam scheduled for later in January, I decided not to make an earlier appointment. After all, if you simply ignore things, they go away--don't they?

Just ten days later, Allen received an amazing series of visions. This is how he described them:

> "Just as I was going to sleep last night, I saw several images. The first was of a present, wrapped in a shiny, mauve-colored foil paper. The box was tied with dark blue and purple ribbons, but these appeared to be squeezing the box, as though it was either wrapped too tightly, or whatever was inside had expanded! Next was an image of a forked branch, one fork slightly smaller than the other one. Both segments of the branch had been cut off close to the fork, and behind it was a spider's web. Third, I saw what looked like an opened Bible, the left-hand page having two columns. The words *"Chapter 13"* began partway down the right-hand column, and there was another break, as though a new chapter were starting, almost at the end of that same column. The page also extended downward, past the edge of the book, to form the shape of a knife or sword blade."

When we anxiously inquired of the Lord, He explained that all three images made up one message. I was shaken by His next words: *"You wouldn't listen, but you must trust."* However, a heartening reminder followed: *"You are being called."*

My mind flew back to that haunting page from Come Away My Beloved. Though I scarcely understood these words and images, I was frightened. Part of me tried to push them out of my mind or rationalize them away, while the other part was driven to try to grasp their meaning. It would be months before I would look back and realize that the swelling box had no doubt been me, while the ribbons represented my tightening waistband! The spider's web, meanwhile, may have exposed

Satan's wicked plan to "cut us off," a biblical term meaning, most literally, to kill us. After all, Jesus Himself had said, "The thief comes only to steal and kill and destroy; I have come that they may have life, and have it to the full." (John 10:10 NIV) However, we were to trust in the sword of God's Word, which promised victory and protection. It was also possible to see in the knife or sword a surgical scalpel. The open book may simultaneously have represented our own lives, while the *"Chapter 13"* notation could also have hinted at the "bankruptcy" of our pursuits, and our lack of trust. Then again, the citation may have pointed to I Corinthians, Chapter 13, and St. Paul's soaring treatise on self-giving love. But also present, almost at the end of that column, was the start of a new chapter, perhaps signaling a new beginning in our lives.

The 30th of December brought this vision. Allen wrote, "I saw a map in my mind, seen as though from high above it. There were two land masses separated by a strait, and at the head of the strait was a golden line reaching across it and well into each land mass." As a strait, according to the dictionary, is also a "position of difficulty, distress, or need," the Lord seemed to be assuring us that He would provide a way across; that He Himself was the golden line bridging the turbulent waters of our lives.

On January 4th, two intriguing scriptures were given. In Jeremiah 13 the prophet was commanded to act out in the physical a message of warning from the Lord, who often resorted to this device when His people had failed to listen to His words alone. The prophets' bizarre symbolic actions made strong visual impressions, and also served to arouse curiosity, thereby increasing the likelihood that the warnings of judgment would be heeded. It seems abundantly clear, in retrospect, that the Lord was intent on getting *my* attention, as well, for my physical symptoms would prove to be an amazingly accurate reflection of my emotional and spiritual life. How often do our physical ailments mirror the *dis*-ease in our souls!

The second scripture, II Corinthians 4:11, seemed to underscore this very theme: "For we who are alive are always being given over to death for Jesus' sake, so that his life may be revealed in our mortal body." (NIV)

In a most remarkable way, the Lord's sanctifying work was being made tangibly evident in my own body, even as I was simultaneously being given over to the possibility of physical death. Because I was weak and vulnerable, my dependence on the Lord's power in the midst of suffering would serve to glorify God, intensify my own spiritual growth, and give testimony to others.

On January 8th of 1992, Allen made this entry in his journal: "This evening, Jan and I were praying for direction and for help and blessing from the Lord in our ongoing struggle with our roles in life. I saw a portion of a dial, with only the number 8 visible, and the hand pointing to a little above it."

This image, as is typically the case, may have had several possible meanings. First, the date of our prayer was obviously *January 8th.* This called to mind the Lord's scriptural admonition against anxiety over the future: "Therefore do not worry about tomorrow, for tomorrow will worry about itself. Each day has enough trouble of its own." (Matt. 6:34 NIV) Hence, by showing that the hand on the dial was pointing to the 8, the Lord may simply have been saying, "Today is the eighth. Let today's troubles be sufficient for today. Do not fret unduly about the future." Surely He was right. We had more than we could do to manage one day's struggles! But the number 8 is also the Biblical number of new beginnings, rebirth, hope, and promise--and this facet of its significance was soon to be manifested in a most interesting way.

Several days later, I asked the Lord again about the timing of the possible trip to Israel with our friend, for I really wanted to go. But I also had an ulterior motive, for surely the Lord's affirmation of that trip would indicate that I had no serious health problem. His answer was only *"You will get a sign."* When I pressed the issue further, His curt and oblique reply was, *"Do what you must."* I had an immediate sense that I was pushing my own will in the matter, but that He would allow it, even at my own peril, and so I quickly abandoned the thought.

However, several days later, while asking for understanding about the Lord's *earlier* words on this matter, Allen wrote this:

> "Last night we prayed about going to Israel, particularly remembering that the Lord had said to let Him lead. I saw a flower of a pale yellow color, with the center nearly the same shade, but a little darker. When we looked that up in an encyclopedia this morning, the sunflower seemed to best fit the description. The book went on to mention that the *Jerusalem* artichoke was a type of yellow sunflower--something we hadn't known!

I caught the Lord's humor, and knew that He was assuring us that we *would* make the trip at some future time. I also saw that he had given me reassurance about my ultimate wellbeing. Now, given the flower image, and with the growing awareness that this trial was not unto physical death, but rather unto new spiritual life, I was encouraged to ask the Lord once more if we should think about a trip to Israel at some later time. He replied, *"Start preparing!"* I later realized that my friend's group would have departed for their tour just two days before my surgery. It was sobering to know that the Lord would have allowed me to have my own way concerning the timing, despite the serious risk to my health. I had managed to hear and obey the Lord's words of warning on this occasion, but how often, I wondered, had the clamor of my own desires drowned out His subtle voice?

Meanwhile, just two days prior to my initial doctor's visit, I had a most odd, and in some ways quite comical dream which I was riding through a series of suburban roads on a blue hippopotamus! Was this bizarre activity reflecting the absurdity and emptiness of my life? I had felt for the last several years that our living situation was neither satisfying our intellectual and spiritual hunger nor suiting our need to be in a more closely-knit spiritual community. True to our pattern, however, our inertia overruled, and so we had done little to seek out other circumstances or opportunities. I also remembered having seen small figurines of blue hippopotami, painted in an azure blue lacquer, in the Egyptian section of several museums. Was the Lord calling me to come out of the "Egypt" of my worldly anxieties and attachments? Was this another dimension of my, and our, bondage?

The next portion of my healing adventure began in earnest on January 27, the date of my routine annual visit to my gynecologist. I had felt more or less fine going into the exam, despite the fact that for the two previous months I had experienced that puzzling sensation of hardness or tension directly behind and around my navel. It was likely due, I kept trying to convince myself, to that extra exercise, though, recently, the swelling and pressure had seemed to increase noticeably. My self-delusion was instantly shattered, when, at the end of the exam, the doctor scheduled an ultrasound to determine the source of what he described as tightness over my left ovary, most probably caused, he said, by an ovarian cyst.

Allen and I were set to leave to visit family in Florida two days later, and so I pushed the looming ultrasound out of my mind, trying to focus instead on the anticipation of the trip. After all, I knew several friends who had lived for periods of time with small, painless ovarian cysts, with no ill effects.

However, as though picking up the theme of our newly heightened medical anxiety, our time in Florida, rather than offering the anticipated warmth, sunshine, and relaxation, was fraught with stress. Allen spent most of the week there battling the remains of a nasty bout of the flu and bronchitis, the weather was mostly chilly and rainy, and each call home to check on Allen's car business was met with aggravating reports of collapsed deals and mechanical disasters.

In the midst of this, thankfully, the Lord continued to give encouragement. The night before our return home, as my mind inevitably began to focus in again on the ultrasound awaiting me, the Lord gave us I Corinthians 2:9: "However, as it is written: 'No eye has seen, no ear has heard, no mind has conceived what God has prepared for those who love him.'" (NIV) It was a marvelous promise in light of what was looming ahead.

When we got back from Florida on Friday night, February 7th, Allen wrote,

> "Back home again! There was a phone call and letter for Jan, each telling her to call Dr. Charles' office with the results of her annual tests. Needless to say, that has caused us both to worry, since we got in too late to call tonight. It seems we have been under attack from Satan for the last two weeks. I believe that the Lord will take care of us if we trust and serve Him, but I sometimes wonder if He doesn't nudge us out of our lethargy by helping us to see what is truly important in our lives. We've had a lot of opportunity in the last several weeks to think about what's important."

In hindsight, I would add that frustrating and difficult circumstances are not necessarily attacks from the Enemy. They may also be the Lord's way of getting our attention.

That same night, the Lord showed Allen this vision:

> "As we continued to pray for the Lord's will for us to be clear, and also asked for forgiveness for our lack of trust, I saw a small pine tree that then changed into a beautiful and perfectly shaped evergreen."

In this striking image, the Lord pointed out that we are daily being changed into His likeness, for our perfecting is His unswerving goal. But we also know that, without sharing in His suffering, this process of sanctification cannot be accomplished, for it is that very sharing that effects it. The little pine tree could only become the perfect evergreen through lifelong spiritual pruning and discipline. In fact, since the evergreen is a symbol of eternal life, the Lord was also reminding us that this challenging and painful process would only be completed when believers are finally glorified in heaven with Him.

Along with this pine tree image came Gal. 4:3, a verse that brought me back to the vision of myself as a child in that dark and forbidding forest: "So also, when we were children, we were in slavery under the basic principles of the world." (NIV) As we cried out in prayer, the Lord gave us another scripture--and one, amazingly, that dealt with the same theme: "Because the patriarchs were jealous of Joseph, they sold him as a slave into Egypt, but God was with him and rescued him from all his troubles." (Acts 7:9-10a NIV) I read these two verses several times before I felt their impact. Joseph had suffered bondage, in part, at the hands of his own family, but God had delivered him and used it all for good. Joseph's story would in several ways come to parallel my own.

Meanwhile, despite the Lord's consolations, and since I could not call the doctor's office until Monday morning, I spent the entire weekend in a state of high anxiety, wondering what could possibly be wrong. When I was finally able to call, I was informed that, in addition to the presumed cyst, I also had two other pelvic infections. With symptoms and issues piling up, it was becoming clear that something was terribly wrong.

If I still had any doubt as to what the Lord was saying to me in all of this, His message on the morning before the ultrasound would bring confirmation, comfort, and encouragement, for Allen heard the sung words of this scripture from Romans 8:28: "So for those who love God, who are called to His plan, everything works out for good." (from the song "Romans 8" by Enrico Garzilli) I have always found, as I ponder those words, that I must resist the temptation to take a *false* and easy comfort from them, for the Lord does not promise that He will prevent adversities from befalling us. Rather, by His grace, He promises to give, *in the midst of* our tribulations, blessings. Indeed, if we are listening, we will in time come to recognize that the tribulations *were* the blessings. This redemptive suffering is at the core of His perfecting work.

Later that night, as we prayed again, the Lord gave Allen these two visions:

"I saw a number of small, white whirlwinds or tornadoes that appeared, and then disappeared, one at a time. These were followed by an image of a dark, round object which was entered from the top by a flowing white substance that poured down around its inside edge, gradually engulfing the dark spot in the center."

The first of these images seemed to affirm the Lord's vigorous healing activity on my behalf. The second also seemed to promise healing, but in a way that was more pictorially accurate that we could, at the time, understand.

On the following day, February 11th, I underwent the ultrasound, still clinging to the hope that nothing was seriously wrong, but I became greatly alarmed by the thinly disguised concern of the examining nurse. After the test, the head nurse called Allen and I aside and explained with medical detachment that the procedure had revealed a large pelvic mass. I was gripped with the greatest fear and despair I had ever experienced. I was next ushered into the lab, where I was given a blood test for cancer, which would come back negative. However, as a result of the ultrasound, I was also scheduled for a CAT scan to further determine the nature and composition of the mass.

The next evening, we stopped to have supper with friends and, after the meal, they suddenly produced a belated Christmas gift: John and Paula Sandfords' book The Elijah Task: A Call to Today's Prophets and Intercessors. I opened the book at random, and my eyes fell directly on these words:

The young man (of Luke 9: 59, 60) wanted to stay at home until his father died, in order that he might perform the filial duty of burying him. Then he would be free to leave home to follow the Lord. But the call of the Lord supersedes family ties. "If any one comes to me and does not hate his own father and mother and wife and children and brothers and sisters, yes, and even his own life, he cannot be my disciple (Luke 14:26 RSV). The Lord of love does not command us to hate in the usual sense. The word means, in this context, a cutting free, a hating of continuing carnal influence. When we accept Jesus Christ as Lord and Savior, that is *a dying to that womb and a new birth into a new life of joy in Him. If we fail to cut the umbilical cord,* (italics mine)...all the inner urges--come nearly unchecked into our new life in Christ, masked under seeming goodness."

Stunned, I closed the book, and randomly opened it again. This time, I read the following:

"Often a counselor's work is to set people free from each other. Idolatry can be very deeply entrenched in family relationships and it must be broken. We need to be separated from each other's unconscious demands, which is why Jesus said He had come not to bring peace but to divide by a sword (Luke 12: 52, 53). When a person falls into the earth and dies--daily--he dies more and more to his own idolatries, as well as to those imposed upon him by others. He thus becomes free *from* others, and free to be *to* them." (pp. 64, 65)

There was that rich sword imagery again. When we shared what we had been experiencing, it was our friends' turn to be stunned. It became clear to all of us that their gift couldn't have been timelier and more profoundly appropriate. It was as though God Himself had handed it to us. But, of course, in His way of things, He had.

For the next few weeks, as I endured a series of difficult pre-operative tests, the Lord continued His messages of hope and healing. On one occasion, He gave the image of a ribbon with a pattern on it. I sensed that the ribbon represented my life, and the pattern, God's intentional design upon it.

On February 21st, the Lord gave me not only a further promise of healing, but also an assignment! These came in the context of Isaiah 38:9, which reads: "A writing of Hezekiah king of Judah after his illness and recovery" (NIV). When I first read this verse, my heart leapt at the words *"after"* and *"recovery."* I *was* going to live! But I read the verse again and realized that I had also been given a clear and unmistakable commission for, in the Lord's divine economy, He desires that nothing, no lesson, go to waste. All healing is ultimately meant to edify *others*, as well, and it is always for a purpose beyond itself. It would be a full year, however, before I would be emotionally able to follow these instructions and begin to write about my experience.

During that same week, I also had three fascinating dreams that would give me not only further insight into my emotional life, but also hope and encouragement concerning my physical and emotional healing, and our future.

In the first, I was in a house with my mother. I was eating a cookie, and decided I needed something to drink. I went to a refrigerator and took out a cardboard half-gallon container of milk (a common symbol of motherly nurturing), but I was suddenly aware of an oddly colored piggy bank on the table. Then I seemed to have a slightly puzzle-shaped object in my hand, which I was required by my mother to deposit in the slot in the piggy bank before I could have the milk. In the dream I felt angry and hurt.

I next dreamt that Allen and I were at some sort of camp or resort. There were many friends there from church. We explored the rooms in the main lodge for a while, and then I became aware that a meal was being prepared in our honor. We were seated beside each other outside on lawn chairs. The meal or banquet seemed to be preparatory to or part of some kind of commissioning for service. There was almost a sense that we were being remarried, or starting our lives with each other in a new way.

The third dream came shortly after receiving the doctor's report regarding the ultrasound. I dreamt I was in our bedroom, and a tri-colored, brown, black, and cream-colored spider, threatening, appeared and began to come toward me. I ducked away from it, and it ran under the bed covers. I lifted them up, down to the mattress pad, and I could see the form of the spider underneath it, but it now seemed smaller and flatter. It continued to run across the bed and over the edge, almost seeming to disappear, or become non-existent.

The following day, I asked the Lord about the next steps in this whole healing process, and He gave us Numbers 2:1. Our Good News Bible was sitting on the coffee table, and it was in this translation that I read, "The Lord gave Moses and Aaron the following instructions." "Lord," I naturally asked, "do you have some specific instructions for us?" There was no further reply. I had no idea what these "instructions" might be, but I felt certain that they would come shortly. The image that followed the verse was that of a sheer cliff with a narrow but brightly-lit path reaching halfway up its side. I was finding the healing task to be arduous, indeed seemingly insurmountable but, with God's help, I was beginning to make progress.

As it happened, I then prayed specifically about going to see two Christian nutritionists in New York State whom friends at church had been strongly urging us to contact, and, as I did so, Allen saw an arrow pointing upward. That image was immediately followed by Revelation 2:7b: To him who overcomes, I will give the right to eat from the tree of life, which is in the paradise of God. (NIV)

My dictionary defined *overcome*: "to get the better of in a struggle or conflict; conquer; defeat, to prevail over, to gain the victory." Clearly, as I have described, the battle, from the beginning, had its source in that arduous but necessary *spiritual* climb, and would be resolved in and through it. The physical manifestations were simply the outward signs of that intense inner struggle. I might also add that one could see the

Lord's subtle humor in the connection between eating, the tree of life, and the two nutritionists.

As we continued to pray, I went on to mention my father, and the Lord immediately responded with the word *"complicity."* Instantly, a veil was lifted, and I was made painfully aware that I had been in lifelong denial about this unfortunate reality, for I had always wanted to see my generally easy-going and even-tempered father as passive, but benign with regard to the family dynamic. This blindness on my part was perhaps largely due to the fact that my mother's issues had so dominated the emotional landscape that I wasn't able see the back side of that mountain. But, perhaps providentially, that blindness was also a protection that my childhood had needed. One dysfunctional parent was more than enough for a young child to deal with. All of this was further complicated by the fact that I was, as I have said, an *only* child, and one who loved both of her parents enormously. After all, none of this could have hurt so much if I hadn't loved them so much, for I was unable to simply walk away, *either emotionally or physically*. But this fact left me feeling even more helpless in the face of the difficulties. I do not mean to suggest that things were always awful, for that was not true. In many ways, I had a great childhood and adolescence, and I always retained a high spirit of adventure, largely instilled by those same parents. But also, as is often the case, my parents' issues, and thus also their behaviors, had become magnified with age. This poignant journal entry captures the emotional dynamic that lay at the root of my ongoing internal battle with it all. I wrote, "I visited my mother in the nursing home yesterday, and was surprised that she remembered my birthday today, and my age. She tried to put her arms around my neck, and said, 'I wish I could do more for you and Daddy.' Often she seems so confused and self-obsessed, and yet she still periodically breaks through into her old self." But now, I also had to face the reality that my father's passivity had not simply been gentle neutrality, but was, rather, its own odd form of abuse, since he had often failed to protect me, *both emotionally and physically*, from my mother's sporadically violent and irrational outbursts. The Lord also wanted me to see *this* situation for what it was, for surely I had carried deeply buried resentment, and this, too, needed to be brought into the light in order to be healed.

On the 26th of February, I received the results of the CAT scan, which revealed that I had not one, but three large pelvic masses. (I am reminded of my dream about the tri-colored spider). I was told I needed a complete hysterectomy. We agreed with the doctor on a surgery date of March 28th, but he called the next day to re-schedule for April 1st. It was a date I would later come to realize was more than coincidence, and not a little amusing, considering its implications! Again we saw that if, even in the midst of crisis, the Lord could have a sense of humor, then so could we!

By this time, I was experiencing further abdominal swelling and pressure, though I continued to have no pain. I did, however, find that I was having increasing difficulty bending over, since that movement was now producing the odd and disturbing sensation that my ribs or my diaphragm were hitting up against something quite large, solid, and substantial. But the Lord was close at hand.

When I asked again about the Numbers 2:1 verse regarding "instructions," and about the Lord's will concerning any other treatments, Allen reported seeing something that resembled a "Y", but all three arms were of equal length and came together with a black dot in the center. As always, our job was simply to record, trusting that the meaning of this enigmatic symbol would become clear shortly.

The following morning, just as I was awakening, I had an extraordinary and unforgettable vision. Here is how I described it:

> "As I was lying in bed, I saw an oven door open, and a rack slid out a little ways. As this happened, there was a bright ball of light inside the oven that moved forward but remained inside. It seemed to flare even more brightly, so that I couldn't quite look at it."

Indeed, the light blazed so intensely that it hurt my eyes, and I literally had to turn my head and look away. I knew that the Lord was assuring me that the image was from Him, and was not something coming from my own imagination.

I felt a great sense of peace, for I knew He was telling me three things. First, since an oven is often used as a symbol of the womb, I believed He was indicating that His light had filled my abdomen, and that the surgery would not only deal with the masses, but would also reveal that I had been fully protected. Second, an oven, like a furnace, is a place for purifying and refining. Hence, the Lord, I somehow knew, was further promising that I, as the ball of light, would come forth shining more brightly than before. Third, this also seemed to be an image of a birthing, recalling the word *"nascent."* I now saw that this referred not only to the growing masses that would be removed, but also to the insight that I was giving birth to my own new self, for I was beginning to learn to give myself permission to *be* myself. The image may also have been an allusion to the future adoption of our three children, as well as to the numerous other children whom the Lord would graciously bring into our lives. Meanwhile, I was still in the midst of a strange and agonizing battle.

On March 1st, as we were in prayer before going to church and then on to a day of visiting with my parents, Allen wrote: "The questions related to Jan seeing her parents today are bothering her. She still feels the anger whenever we plan to go there, but she also feels guilty about not seeing them."

For years, I had dealt with a miserable mixture of anger and guilt, and I longed to be free of it. It was becoming clear to me that I desperately needed healing--not only physically, but emotionally and spiritually, as well, from the wounds experienced during the course of my life. As I asked the Lord *how* I was to proceed through this inner healing struggle, Allen thought he heard the words *"help others."* Once again, I was being exhorted to forget myself by immersing myself in acts of service, worship, and community--by *giving*--for the Lord knows these are the best medicine. This was followed by the Greek word *"koinonos,"* meaning, "companions, those who partake together at the altar." The Lord was also reminding me that I had *received* and would continue to *receive* tremendous love, healing, and support from many good friends at our church.

On this same date, we were also surprised to finally receive the previously promised "instructions" of Numbers 2:1 for which we had been anxiously waiting! These came in the form of the following two scriptures: "Then the word of the Lord came to me:" (Jeremiah 16:1 NIV), and "Please test your servants for ten days: Give us nothing but vegetables to eat and water to drink." (Daniel 1:12 NIV) These verses confirmed that we were most definitely being called to make the three-hour trip to see the two nutritionists whom our friends had recommended.

March 4th was Ash Wednesday and, after the evening service at church, I went forward to the altar rail for prayer. As Allen and our pastor laid hands on me and began to pray, Allen was given I Corinthians 1:17-20: "For Christ did not send me to baptize, but to preach the gospel-- not with words of human wisdom, lest the cross of Christ be emptied of its power. For the message of the cross is foolishness to those who are perishing, but to us who are being saved it is the power of God. For it is written: 'I will destroy the wisdom of the wise; the intelligence of the intelligent I will frustrate.' Where is the wise man? Where is the scholar? Where is the philosopher of this age? *Has not God made foolish the wisdom of the world?*" (NIV italics mine)

I saw here an obvious exhortation to mission and ministry--but also, curiously, one that was being placed in the context of a certain specific but yet-to-be discerned wisdom! To our great surprise, the meaning of that latter theme would shortly be revealed in a most unexpected way.

Now, with a little over three weeks until my surgery, the Lord's messages began to intensify. On March 6th, as I continued to ask Him for healing, He replied, *"There are reasons."* The word was veiled and subtle. Nonetheless, I felt I understood Him to mean that there were unknown and complex reasons--not only for my illness--but also for the things He had chosen to allow, and the ways in which He would direct my healing. The word was also clear enough to make me understand that there were other issues in my life that the Lord was beginning to address. It was as if He were saying, "And, while we're at it..." His timing was perfect, for He certainly had my full attention! Suffice it to say that nothing escapes His scrutiny and judgment. But God is good, for His desire is not to hurt us, but to make us whole--to bring *shalom.*

I also asked the Lord if there was anything I might do to assist in my own healing. *"Pennae,"* was the response. On checking, I discovered that the word, from the Latin, is the plural of *"penna,"* meaning "pen, quill, writing instrument." Here was yet another exhortation to write. The same word is also used for a bird's wing and tail feathers, *from which* these writing implements were for so long made. Here, I believe, was a second and subtle message for, in retrospect, two of the greatest aids in my healing process had been writing and "migrating": *packing up* and going to a new location, not only physically, but emotionally, and spiritually, as well.

Meanwhile, as we continued to seek His guidance, asking one more time regarding going to see the nutritionists, He replied, *"All things are possible with those who love the Lord."* Allen then described the following: "I saw several lumpy white shapes on top of a dark shape, and then they disappeared, and a bright, white leaf floated downward." This prompted me to ask if it were really the Lord's will that I should have surgery, and Allen heard the words, *"Remember, trust and explore."* I was left pondering whether it might be the Lord's desire to heal me solely through the nutritional fasting and retreat process, thereby making the surgery unnecessary, or if that process was simply one facet of a larger work. My best discernment at the time obviously led me to opt for the surgery. Sometime later, when I began to write about this whole experience, I again brought the issue before the Lord. First, He replied, *"I put doctors on earth for a reason."* He then added, *"What good would it do for you to know?"* When I protested that I needed to understand in order to explain to others, He continued, *"You don't have to have a reason for everything. That's My job."* Then He reminded me, *"You are to relate, but not to speculate."*

On March 7th we drove out to see the nutritionists, and I was tested and evaluated. To our astonishment, these two wonderful women explained their recommendation this way. After testing, they said, most people could be sent home with a nutritional protocol. However, my tests had revealed such alarming results that they immediately prescribed a *ten-day*, closely supervised bed retreat in their home. It would begin with a *strict fast*, the first few days of which would allow only *water* with lemon juice! This would then be followed with added *vegetable juices* and soups! During the full time, I was also to be *re-tested* several times daily, and would also be *supervised* round the clock. I would be, as it were, under guard! Their *simple* yet *powerful* healing prescription matched almost identically the text from Daniel! Equally astonishing was the fact that their logo was a "Y", enclosed in a circle, symbolizing the coming together of the physical, emotional, and spiritual dimensions of healing! To our further surprise, and just as we were about to leave, they unexpectedly quoted I Corinthians 1:27 to us: *"But God chose the foolish things of the world to shame the wise; God chose the weak things of the world to shame the strong."* (NIV) It was yet another sign that we were in the right place at the right time and doing the right thing. We saw that the Lord delights in demonstrating His power and watchful care in the face of seemingly impossible odds, and, since repetition is emphasis, we should certainly have been getting a clearer insight into God's will and His purposes.

The following day, a sometimes forgotten aspect of the Lord's nature was revealed when He gave us Joshua 7:9. There Joshua pleads with the Lord to give His people victory over the pagan Amorites, and His argument was as follows: "The Canaanites and the other people of the country will hear about this and they will surround us and wipe out your name from the earth. What then will you do for your own great name?" As my NIV Bible text note explained, "God's honor in the eyes of all the world was at stake in the fortunes of His people." Among other reasons, God seemed to be suggesting that He would heal me for the sake of His own reputation and, what's more, was actually *encouraging* me to plead my case before Him on that basis!

These motifs repeated again on March 9th with a number of words and visions from the Lord. First, Allen reported that he felt led to lay hands on me and pray. As he did so, he saw an opening into a dark area filled with little white streaks. The Lord then seemed to be telling him to call on the power of Christ's cross to go in and light up the darkness. Allen immediately had a sense of seeing a sparkling, luminescent light in his field of vision, and he next heard the words, "*There is power in the blood.*" A reference to psalm 23 followed. I had read the psalm many times since childhood, but, now, I was agonizingly aware of my *own* sojourn "in the valley of the shadow of death." (v. 4) The Lord then added, *"And read Psalm 22 while you're at it!"* From the cross, Jesus had quoted the first verse: "My God, my God, why have you forsaken me? Why are you so far from saving me, so far from the words of my groaning?" (NIV) In Jewish tradition, the first verse of a psalm alludes to the entire psalm, and psalm 22 ends triumphantly. Thus, I sensed that Jesus was reminding me, not only, of His unmerited suffering on my behalf, *but also of His ultimate victory*, which I saw as a promise of my own healing.

On March 12th, the Lord stressed again the significant role of spiritual gifts in my healing process, giving us I Corinthians 12:1: "Now about spiritual gifts, brothers, I do not want you to be ignorant." (NIV) He seemed to be saying that He would be using my whole healing experience as a teaching vehicle concerning the gifts of the Holy Spirit.

I then prayed one last time about the trip to the nutritionists, asking the Lord if I was being foolish in doing the 10-day retreat. He responded with Isaiah 22:10, which gave us some interesting insights into the fasting regimen that I was about to begin: "You counted the buildings in Jerusalem and *tore down houses to strengthen the wall.*" (italics mine) We were, at first, baffled by the significance of this verse, in light of my question! But Allen realized that it gave a fairly accurate physiological description of what happens when the body fasts! He next described seeing a road running between two wire fences. We understood Him to be saying, "I will safeguard your journey. Your way is protected. Go in confidence." With that, my mind was fully made up, and I made preparations to go on my ten-day fast and retreat.

Allen drove me to New York on the 14th of March, and he would return for me on the 24th. While I was gone from home, he prayed for me nightly. On my second evening away, he felt he heard the Lord tell him to read Jeremiah 17:7: "But blessed is the man who trusts in the Lord, whose confidence is in him." (NIV) Clearly, we had shown enough trust to engage the process, but trust also remained the area in which we most needed to grow, and we were certainly being given ample opportunity to do so. After all, there is really no perceived need to trust if everything seems to be going just fine.

On the fourth night of my retreat, I had a most interesting experience. As I had every night since the fasting process began, I awakened at about 4:30 A.M. feeling dizzy and queasy. But on this night, when I fell back to sleep, I had the following dream:

> "I dreamed that I was standing in front of a washing machine. The lid was up, and I was watching the rinse cycle spin round and round. Then, as I watched the spinning, my mother came up behind me and grabbed me from the back in a playful way, as she once might have done."

I later wrote, "On waking, I felt that the rinsing and spinning of the machine represented the flushing and cleansing of my system through the fasting process, and it also explained that the dizziness was from the detoxifying." My mother's presence was also highly significant, for so much of my inner healing was centered on my relationship with her. It was all somehow interconnected.

I would later come to realize that there had been several purposes for the retreat. First, it had physically strengthened and prepared me for the surgery, and it would also contribute much to my recovery process. A second, and unexpected, blessing was that I was able to soak up and internalize ten intense days of nurturing, motherly care. Third, I myself would go on to become trained in the testing procedure, thereby helping others as well.

On March 25th, the day after my return home, and the evening before my pre-operative appointment, we prayed again--this time, about my worries over not having had the emotional energy to donate my own blood, as a suggested precaution in the event of a transfusion. Allen had a vision of a misty veil of gold dropping down from above, as though a blessing were falling, and he heard the words, *"Thou, O Lord, art a shield about me."* It was true: Dr. Charles later reported that I had lost very little blood, thereby making a transfusion unnecessary.

It was now March 31st, the day before my surgery. That morning, Allen wrote:

> "Jan and I were talking and praying this morning--really dealing with some issues of fear, and the guidance of the Lord. As we did so, I saw a large 'X'.""As I watched, the 'X' seemed to be stationary, but also moving, as though the 'X' and I were moving together in relation to the rest of the world. Then I heard the phrase, *'Do not be faithless, only believe,'* pointing us to the words of Jesus to Jairus, whose daughter lay dead. (See Mark 5:36) Again at noon we prayed. Jan asked to get healed, so that she can get on with her life. As I closed my eyes, I saw a flash of purple, followed by a white arch with a large 'X' across the archway."

The Greek letter *X* is the first letter in the word *Christos*, or Christ, and the color purple conveyed the Lord's majesty, as well as His Passion, while the arch showed that He would make the way, and indeed was the Way. I especially liked the idea of Jesus and me moving together, in union and harmony, against the backdrop of the world. But in hind-sight, I also see that the whole healing process that I was undergoing at the time *was* my life, not an interlude, interruption, annoyance or distraction. It was the necessary preparation for the next steps, and not something to get past in order to get on with "the real stuff." St. Paul said it well: "Set your minds on things above, not on earthly things. For you died, and your life is now hidden with Christ in God." (Colossians 3:2-3 NIV)

I continued in prayer, repenting of what seemed my characteristic lack of trust, and Allen heard the Lord say, *"You're not bad."* Here was a statement that spoke volumes, for the voice of my damaged childhood emotions had continually informed me that I was being punished and, no doubt, deservedly so. The Lord later suggested, *"Surely you can share."* He was already telling us to look beyond the surgery to the opportunities we would have to tell the good news, to "make known among the nations what he has done." (I Chronicles 16:8 NIV) Most extraordinary and memorable of all was the last image given. It was that of the V-shaped corner of a corral fence. Its blessed meaning would shortly be clear.

Finally, the dreaded date of April 1st arrived, and I arose early, numb with fear. I remember wistfully taking off my rings, including my wedding ring, and placing them in my jewelry box just before we set off for the hospital. I clung desperately to the words and images we had been given, but a part of me wondered if I would ever get to wear them again. I was scheduled to be there at 6 A.M. I remember arriving at the surgical center, and being escorted to a partitioned room where I changed into a hospital gown, and then sat on a gurney, once more shaking from fright. After some time, we were again escorted, this time to the pre-operative room, where I was to await my turn in the line-up. There were two rows of occupied gurneys against the walls of this room, and I remember scanning each face to see if anyone else was as petrified as I. No one seemed to be. At length, a nurse appeared with an I.V., and I remember her giving my hand a numbing shot before she inserted the needle. I had requested a sedative, and so that immediately followed. I remember nothing else.

I was wheeled into the operating room, as scheduled, at 7 A.M. My next recollection is that of a kindly nurse bending over me and repeating, "Jan! Jan! Wake up! It's all over!" I smiled through my pain, and promptly fell back to sleep. The next time I woke, it was to see Dr.

Charles standing over me, but the only words I remember were these: "You have cancer." The next twelve hours are marked in my memory only by the 4-hour points at which I received my morphine shots. And so passed that first day.

The morning of the day after the surgery, I awakened to disquieting news. Here is Allen's journal entry from later that afternoon:

> "Jan had surgery yesterday, and was extremely nervous going into it. I waited at the hospital for what seemed an incredibly long time. The surgery was more extensive than we had hoped. Dr. Charles found a large cystic mass, the size of a man's head, which was benign. It was wrapped around two other cysts, the larger of which was benign, but the smaller of which was on the ovary, and in an early stage of cancer, as nearly as he and the oncologist could tell. They did a complete hysterectomy, removed the omentum (the intestinal lining), did a pelvic wash, and also took lymph node samples. We are awaiting the results of those tests in prayer and faith that the Lord has a good plan for both of us in this. We have been blessed by the love and support of our church family and of our Christian friends. I feel lifted up by the prayer and concern, and I know it has to help Jan. I am a little concerned about her attitude, but, whatever happens, I know we must put our trust in Jesus."

When Allen and I were next able to pray together, it was on April 7th, the evening before my post-operative exam and biopsy report. He wrote, "Jan is healing from the major surgery last Wednesday, and we are waiting for the last of the three test results regarding the cancer. The first two were very good, but we have one more, which we will find out about tomorrow morning at nine." He continued, "As we prayed about the final test result, I saw the image of a circle of white, with an angled cross inside of it." The veracity of this assurance of complete healing, and of its divine origin, were again reinforced by I Corinthians 2:13: "This is what we speak, not in words taught us by human wisdom but in words taught by the Spirit, expressing spiritual truths in spiritual words." (NIV) The Lord knew that at this critical time I especially needed assurance that the message was indeed from Him, and that it did speak of my total deliverance.

We then prayed for a complete healing, and Allen saw a vision of a thick wooden pole, wound round with a heavy rope. The Lord seemed to be saying that I had been lashed to the mast during this storm, and that He Himself was the mast. His closing words to us were *"Blessings and peace to you."*

The next morning, April 8th, found me once more sitting nervously on the examining table in Dr. Charles' office. He strolled in, biopsy reports in hand, and gave us both a large grin. "Here are your pink slips," he said. "You are free to go home and enjoy the rest of your life!" The surgery, he said, had finally revealed two things no one had suspected or imagined. First, while there were in fact three large pelvis masses, they were not separate, as originally believed, but rather *contained one within the other.* Second, the innermost mass, located on the ovary itself, had turned malignant, but was so *completely encapsulated* by the large outer mass that *no malignancy had escaped* into the abdominal cavity. Hence, there were no further traces of cancer to be dealt with.

More interesting still, I even saw the Lord's stamp in the number and configuration of the pelvic masses, for their three-in-one and one-in-three composition had suggested His Trinitarian protection. Now we could look back and realize that the Lord had kept the malignancy *"corralled"* inside the largest, outer cystic mass. I will forever cherish that simple image and what it signified. It also seemed that the *V-shaped* corner of the fence had signified victory. Now, finally, we could see that the surgery date of April 1st had truly been of the Lord--His joke on Satan, perhaps!

The April 8th date of the post-operative exam had also proven to be a most auspicious sign. First, it fell *seven* days after the surgery and, biblically speaking, the number seven stands for covenant. Furthermore, the Lord had already shown from scripture that the number 8 signified new beginnings. For example, we note that the *eight* people in Noah's family were delivered through the Flood to repopulate the earth. Similarly, circumcision of male infants in the Old Covenant was also commanded on the *eighth* day after birth, and baptismal fonts are often in the shape of an octagon, a visual reminder of our "dying" with Christ and rising to new life. St. Paul writes, "Or are you unaware that we who were baptized into Christ Jesus were baptized into his death? We were indeed buried with him through baptism into death, so that, just as Christ was raised from the dead by the glory of the Father, we too might live in newness of life." (Romans 6: 3-4 NAB) There were further intimations as well, though it would be some years before we saw them. I have chosen here to quote from the Catechism of the Catholic Church, since it does a far better job than I could in explaining the profound connections between the dates of my surgery and post-operative exam, and the Lord's greater purposes for me, and for us. From paragraph 2174, it reads: "Jesus rose from the dead 'on the first day of the week.' Because it is the "first day," the day of Christ's Resurrection recalls the first creation. Because it is the "eighth day" following the sabbath, it symbolizes the new creation ushered in by Christ's Resurrection. For Christians it has become the first of all days, the first of all feasts, the Lord's Day--Sunday." And from paragraph 2175, it reads: "In Christ's Passover, Sunday fulfills the spiritual truth of the Jewish sabbath and announces man's eternal rest in God."

For the Church, then, every "first day," every Sunday, is also, in perpetuity, an "8th day." As a celebration of Christ's resurrection, it is a feast, a solemnity, a Passover, and a mini-Easter. It is a day to remember our deliverance from eternal physical and spiritual death, and a day of healing, praise, thanksgiving and worship. It is ever a day of new beginnings. Now I, and we, had been delivered in order to begin *our* new life in the Lord, a life that would ultimately lead us to these realities as celebrated most fully in the sacred Mass. Truly, the Lord had been in charge *from* the beginning!

I left the surgeon's office, half-laughing, and half-crying, and went home to follow his directive. I was indeed *free*: free from cancer and its threat, free from any further treatments, and free to go home and enjoy the rest of my life!

Thus ends the strictly medical portion of my healing adventure. Yet we were also in the process of being freed from much, much more--and no less than a circumcision of our own hearts would be required of us! But that will be the subject of our continuing journey.

In that day you will say:

"*Give thanks* to the Lord, call on his name;

make known among the nations what he has done,

and *proclaim* that his name is exalted.

Sing to the Lord, for he has done glorious things;

let this be known to all the world.

Shout aloud and sing for joy, people of Zion,

for great is the Holy One of Israel among you." (italics mine)

(Isaiah 12:4-6 NIV)

* *

Some time later, having gained a little distance from the immediate trauma of my experience, and following Isaiah's instructions, I was led to enumerate in writing the lessons I had learned and the blessings I had received. Here are my reflections:

1. God's abiding desire for us is "shalom," meaning wholesome integration of mind and spirit, soundness, wellbeing, and the peace that passes understanding. This is at the core of what Jesus meant when He said, "The thief comes only to steal and kill and destroy; *I have come that they may have life, and have it to the full.*"(John 10:10 NIV--italics mine) This does not mean that we are *entitled* to physical healing, but God often uses it to advance His Kingdom.

2. As a corollary, God's desire for each of us is that we come into the

fullness of the calling and ministry for which He has purposed and destined us.

3. In order to accomplish these two things in our lives, the Lord may find it necessary to work through what seem to us difficult circumstances--that is, to afflict us for our greater good. This is neither a pleasant nor a popular thought, but the Lord is a jealous God. When we are called to ministry, to His purposes, He will remove, by violence if necessary, all that competes with our devotion to Him. Some time ago, the Lord gave us the word *"causality,"* which, theologically and philosophically speaking, points to "the end or purpose for which a thing is done." God knows what He is about.

4. Furthermore, scripture clearly teaches that we are called to share with Christ in His sufferings, in order that we may be glorified with Him. Like Job, we will be called to times when we struggle mightily to understand that suffering.

5. God is anxious to demonstrate His power through the administration of His spiritual gifts in His Body, the Church. Furthermore, there is great joy and blessing when believers, having received the Lord's comfort, are able in turn to give comfort to others. Writing is one medium through which others may be helped and healed. It was therefore critically important that we had kept prayer journals, in order to record our experiences, reflections, dreams and visions, and the Lord's words to us. Without that consistent discipline, the sharing of our journey, and of my healing, in particular, would have been well-nigh impossible. I pass this insight along in the form of an exhortation.

6. In many instances, our illnesses contain a symbolic element, having their roots in the emotional and the spiritual dimensions of our being. In my case, the tension surrounding my navel showed the need to cut away from the destructive family bondage rooted in childhood, while the abdominal swelling pointed to the birthing of a new life--my own--as well as, perhaps, to the subconscious desire for children.

7. The promise of Romans 8:28 is this: "We know that all things work for good for those who love God, who are called according to his purpose." (NAB) This does not mean that *only* that which *we perceive* as good will happen to us, but that God will enable *whatever* He allows to happen to us to work for good, for all who believe and trust in Him. Thus, we are encouraged to be at peace, both with His eternal purposes, and with His work in our present circumstances. This word came to me repeatedly in the prayers, phone-calls, letters, and conversations of those who had ministered to us.

8. Much of the time, we are all too able to delude ourselves about our self-reliance and our capacity to control life's situations. But times of severe crisis and distress are God-ordained opportunities to draw closer to Him, for it is then that we need, more than ever, to praise Him, and to trust in Him. We have learned far more from, and been far more blessed by, the challenges and the sufferings, than by the times of ease and comfort. Pain has its place and its role to play. Some time ago, I purchased a bottle of Jamaican hot sauce, and when I reached into the refrigerator to grab the bottle, I noticed these words on the label: "Pain Is Good." Most likely, the makers had not grasped the larger theological message, but God can use anything!

9. In our times of crisis, we also learn to face our deepest fears, and we discover that with the Lord's help, we can not only survive, but emerge stronger. This is always the central purpose behind God's testing.

10. There are costs to our disobedience of the Lord. These may include continued emotional and spiritual bondage, unnecessary mental and physical suffering, a missing of our highest ministry and calling, and a lack of peace--*shalom*.

11. God is serious about the issue of forgiveness. Although Joseph's own brothers sold him into slavery, his forgiveness enabled God to bless them all.

12. We must stay close to the Lord at all times, and we must always

be listening, praying, pondering, and meditating on His Word, but we must be also respond in faith to what we hear in prayer and through other circumstances. When God begins to work through *painful* circumstances, it is sometimes because He has been speaking ever more loudly, and we have failed to heed Him.

13. Finally, I was increasingly conscious of the degree to which my emotional bondage had been of my own doing. Some months after my surgery, I visited with a pastor friend who himself was struggling with cancer, and I told him my story. He summed it all up with these words: "Jan, I think what the Lord was trying to tell you, in today's vernacular, was 'Get a life!'" Instantly, I was brought back to a vision I had had quite some time before. I was in a small, dark prison cell, a place where I had apparently been for a long time, when I suddenly became aware of a narrow beam of light falling from above me, and landing on a spot on the floor. When I glanced down, I saw in the center of the spot of light a key, but I was afraid to reach down and pick it up. I glanced up again, just in time to see the door swinging open from the outside. There in the distance was a beautiful meadow bathed in sunshine, beckoning me forth. I then noticed the Lord, standing to the left of the doorway, His hand still on the door. He bent down, looked in, smiled, and with a mixture of amusement and compassion, He said, *"You can come out, you know."* <u>Much of my life had been spent as a prisoner of my own making, for the key had been there all along.</u>

It would be a full ten years before I began my initial writing of the hysterectomy story, and, as I revisited, pondered, and questioned the journal material from the time of my illness, the Lord had this to say:

> *"The experience was a natural outworking of all that was going on in your life, and it was an opportunity, which you took, to draw closer to Me and to face the hard reality of a necessary change of direction. You actually responded in the*

way that I desired, though you did not, then, and surely do not, even now, understand all of the implications of your choices. I have led you on this path, and I will lead you further. Just as you are amazed now, so you will be further amazed ten years from now. I have good plans for all, but those who listen and obey will have the joy of participating in My plans.

6

Further Thoughts on Healing and Purpose

The following offers some further thoughts, as well as some questions and issues addressed, on the subjects of hearing, healing, and purpose.

Why do we need or want to know more about the process of healing in the context of hearing and purpose, anyway? Let me begin by saying that we are not encouraging those who have health concerns to rely solely on prayer and eschew the doctor. We have neither the right nor the authority to do that. Besides, avoiding the doctor altogether is not the prime purpose of learning to hear the Lord better. As my two stories of healing have shown, the doctors themselves played major roles in helping to fulfill God's greater purposes for me--and, perhaps unwittingly, for themselves, as well, while in the process of restoring me to physical health. We also applaud the fact that there are many fine and selfless doctors, including many who understand the Biblical principles of health and healing and who pray for and with their patients. Furthermore, there are many sad cases of people who died because they simply refused to go to a doctor.

However, as my two stories have shown, healing is often multi-

62

dimensional. Some time ago, while in prayer concerning a friend whom we thought had had a premature and unnecessary death from illness, we heard the Lord say the following:

> *You, cannot, of course, make anyone do anything, except by exercising tyrannical control. I could make people do many, many things that were beneficial for them, but I have chosen to allow each of you to make free choices because I want My people to freely choose Me rather than being obedient little robots. You are correct that your friend could have lived much longer if she had not been so committed to the medical establishment. In that area, her faith was more in them than in Me, though she surely had a saving faith, and is with Me. In the area of health, there are many who wish to cede control to "experts" so that they do not have to be in charge of that part of life. It is somehow comforting to them to think that there is someone with great knowledge looking after them. The problem is that I am speaking to each individual in ways that are personal to them, and doctors only know about groups of people. By the nature of their profession today, doctors, even if they are devoted Christians who pray for their patients, are often driven to use products that "fix' the immediate symptom, though they seldom get to the root cause. Doctors simply cannot do the listening that the individuals must do for themselves. Thus, they can be agents of My grace in a general way but, not in the specific way that is normally required for the true healing which cures the root of the problem, rather than simply mitigating the symptoms. This is a very difficult thing, because most systemic illness has at least a partial source in sin and spiritual problems, so getting at the physical root cause does not deal with those larger issues. However, in the hearing process leading to some significant healing, trust is gained which moves toward the greater healing. The medical establishment, as it exists in the*

modern West, is surely driven by money in much of what it does, and that leads to a strong tendency to "fix the problem" rather than cure the whole physical system. I have made the body in such a way that it is capable of remarkable self-healing if it is properly fed and balanced. I provide all that is necessary for that in the natural world, and you have often received My instruction because you have asked. In this culture, and now in much of the world, natural and healthy foods are being replaced by processed, quick, and addictive (in the case of sugars, fats, and salt) foods that throw the system out of balance and eventually lead to vulnerabilities and a host of diseases. But the mind set of patients and doctors is often to deal with the problem part but not to deal with changes in diet, exercise, and the disciplines which make those things work. There is, certainly, a huge spiritual component to all of this, because abuse of the organism that I created tends to go along with a disregard for My role in all of life. People simply do not want Me to be Lord of their overeating or overindulgence in any area because they instinctively know they'd have to stop. There are some who want Me to be Lord of their Sunday morning "worship" and Bible studies and even their bouts with illness and tragedy, but they don't want Me to be Lord of their questionable practices at work or in their relationships. They don't want Me to be Lord of their diets, their abuse of various beverages and substances, or their conversation. Indeed, this subject gets into most areas of life. People want fixes without healing. The process of healing is painful because it means real change of heart and behavior, and many do not want that at all: "A band aid will do just fine." But I don't do band aids. I do shalom. That's it.

Some questions may naturally arise for the reader in the course of processing *our* stories. For example, why was I physically healed, when others are often not? Is healing a sign of God's favor? Is illness, conversely, a sign of God's disfavor? Was I healed because I was deemed "more deserving," whatever that means? Are others not healed because they don't engage the listening process? What if they don't even know about the process? Are illness and death a sign of God's punishment, or perhaps His presumed lack of love or goodness? What about what *we* would call accidents? What about war, or martyrdom? Scripture informs and reminds us of the fact that we are all living with the natural outworking of the Fall, and we can't change that reality. After all, you can only proceed from where you are, and not from where you wish you had been. But the blessed assurance, the glorious promise, is that God has allowed these things, not only because He respects our free will, but because He has an indescribably greater healing in store for those who trust and believe--that of *eternal* union with Him in the fellowship of the Holy Trinity. After all, He's really, really smart, and He always has the last word! Finally, these questions can only be addressed and answered in the context of each individual's utterly unique and personal relationship with the Lord, in the greater context of His wisdom and His purposes, and all in the context of allowing free will in the face of evil.

Thankfully, the lives of the saints, in scripture and through history, provide some of the best and the most practical insights into these matters. As one example, consider St. Ignatius of Loyola, the proud soldier whose leg was shattered by a cannonball. His agonizing months of bedridden confinement, and his resulting restlessness and boredom, ultimately drove him to read the lives of numerous saints who had gone before. And that, in turn, led to his profound spiritual conversion, to priesthood, to the founding of the Jesuit order, and to an enormous religious and social impact, not only across Europe but, throughout much of the world. Without his suffering, none of the rest would have followed. God's ways are not our ways.

In this context, we offer this word which we thought we heard regarding the difficult questions of why God sometimes *delays* or *denies* healing, and their corollary, that of why He often *allows* illness and suffering:

> *These are secrets I do not reveal. I wish all healed, but most misunderstand healing. I am seeking deeper healing, though sometimes physical healing serves that purpose. I often let the process proceed through human means because a miraculous healing would cause more harm than it would do good. I do heal as a testimony to My Gospel, and I do heal physically when that work will accomplish My greater purposes. I do not choose pain and suffering, for I know too well the agony, but I also know that in many lives these terrible difficulties clear the mind and prepare the soul for eternal life. These are hard things that are not easy to explain. I desire the best for all My children, but often, "best" does not mean a simple human desire for healing, or even abundance. I have good plans, and I will do what is necessary.*

Included here, also, is a fascinating word on how our work interfaces with and cooperates with God's purposes for us and in the wider world:

> *I will do what I do, but you are to do all the things that I have gifted you to do. You cannot do what I do, and I choose not to do what I have trusted My people to do. It is the only way to grow. Trust in Me for all that is impossible for you, but remember that I work through My people's hands, feet and minds. You will have confusion about this: Some of the things you assume only I can do can be accomplished by My people; some of the things you think you can do easily require My power to be accomplished. Submit it all to Me, and ask for wisdom. I have plans. I want My people to know the joy of using all the power and the gifts I have given, and I like-wise want them to be aware of the power which lies at My fingertips when all of their own resources fail. These are hard*

times, yet they are also joyous times. You will be astonished by what I will do, and also by that which I have entrusted to you. I know you have moments of struggle, and that is truly inevitable, but you will also see My plans emerging as a green shoot breaking through the surface of the ground with the promise of growth and abundant fruit. You must simply do your work, and I will do Mine. I will take care of the details, for I'm very good at that sort of thing. Stay in prayer and keep listening. You will see the power of My Holy Spirit move.

We will close this chapter by relating the realization that came to me as I later worked on the editing of these two stories of healing. Yes, Allen and I had indeed prayed and worked our way through that fear-filled and distressing time in our lives relying almost entirely on the Lord's guidance. That guidance, however, was not that of the *fuller words* we have since come to expect on a regular basis, and of which the reader has already had a small taste. Instead, we had relied *solely* on strong nudges, dreams, visions, scripture citations, a few short sentences, and, on occasion, the opportune advice of friends, which we discerned to be the Lord speaking. At the time, of course, we knew of nothing else, and so these things were all we had to go on and to work with. But now, in hindsight, I am *awed* and *amazed* by it all. Looking back, I am *amazed* that we had enough confidence in what we thought we were hearing, nearly all of which was enigmatic and ephemeral, to follow the path of our understandings to obedience and healing. It's all the more remarkable since, the more badly we want to hear, the more prone our hearing can be to our own distortions. Yet, through our trembling obedience and, by God's grace and design, our hearing accomplished what was necessary. Moreover, this blessed reality also allows us to encourage others who may still be at an early point in learning the hearing process. I am also *awed* that God allowed us the incredible honor of risking for a good outcome. That thought utterly astonishes me, for so much--indeed, everything, from our perspective--was at stake. In hindsight, of course, *we know* that He had it all under control, and, knowing the end from the beginning, *He knew* what we would do.

People often ask me why we pay so much attention to dreams, to fleeting images, to threads woven over time, to incidental circumstances, and to the still small Voice. My prayer is that in reading these stories of my, and our, deliverance, the reader has better understood the answer to that question.

Before we continue with the narrative of my, and our, inner healing, and our calls, we will pause to explore our choice of book title. Some time ago, when asking the Lord about His plans concerning our path, we heard the words *"Pack up."* Later, the Lord added, *"There is no retirement in the spiritual life."* It struck me that the essence of the spiritual life--if it is to be fulfilled and fulfilling--and if we are to become who and what we are called to be--must be one of *movement,* of motion, of sometimes falling back, and yet of always straining forward. If both processes are cooperatively engaged, our own lives become living parables.

We see this movement actively at work in the lives of Abraham, who leaves home to go to a land God *will* show him, and of Jacob, whose years-long journey takes him to Haran and back. We see it in Joseph, who is dragged to Egypt against his will, and there becomes not only second in command to Pharaoh, but also the savior of his famine-stricken family. Famine likewise plays a role in the story of Ruth's return to her homeland, there to become the ancestor of another Savior. Again, we read of Moses' sudden distraction by the curious and demanding bush of fire, of the Israelites and their Passover Exodus, and of the Holy Family on their flight to Egypt, and later return to Galilee. Then there is Matthew's call to leave his tax booth, Zacchaeus' descent from the sycamore tree, Peter's hastily dropped nets, and Paul, interrupted and blinded on the road to Damascus, in preparation for crisscrossing the Mediterranean with the message of salvation for Jews and Gentiles alike. Of course, there is also the Samaritan woman at the well, who ran to announce the Messiah and whose life, and many of her neighbors', would never be the same. Then, there is the Way of the Cross: the Passion that every believer is uniquely destined and exhorted to repeat, yet with Christ's promise of a glorious and eternally New Beginning.

Again, sometimes our movement is largely *interior*, as with those many saints or "blesseds" who spent years in monastic cells or in prison cells. Some saints, like St. Therese of Liseux, or Blessed Ann Catherine Emmerich, lived years of their lives confined to a sick bed, where they wrote of their interior spiritual journeys and mesmerized the world. Being human, sometimes our initial movement is not toward God, but away, as with Jonah, but God can and will ultimately use it all. As the above examples illustrate, it is God's way to break in, break through, and interrupt, in order that His divinely ordained will might become our own purpose and our unique destiny, but we must cooperate. Mary's response to Gabriel's announcement was, "May it be done to me according to your word." (Luke 1:38b NAB) It should be ours, as well.

As the Lord has further reminded us:

> *"I know that you want clarity about these things, but you also know that the guidance comes as you are moving in the direction you do know. As you are proceeding, you will find your mind becoming more focused and clearer,and you will understand the next step. The steps don't exist as separate, isolated items, but they run together as a means to fulfill My plans in your life. You, indeed, can't know the full plan at first, because you are not ready. Doing what you know and can do, gets you ready. It's a good plan! I've used it before! Shalom!"*

Yet another beloved spiritual pilgrim, Saint Catherine of Sienna, rightly discerned the true nature of this life's journey, and proclaimed the process both brilliantly and succinctly when she declared, "All the way to heaven is heaven, because Jesus said, 'I am the way.'"

Finally, when, we might ask, does a call begin? The answer almost always is, "Long before we realize it has." And so it would be that our own journey would eventually take us through four years in seminary, ordination to the Episcopal Church priesthood, and a parish in Alabama. We also heard and followed the call to the adoption of our three Russian children, the hosting of thirteen foreign exchange students, priesthood in the Anglican Communion, our journey home to the Catholic Church, our writing, our teaching, and much more. Why did the Lord choose to work in this way? The answer, as noted above, is that He can only lead us to the degree that we are able to hear at the time, and He makes skillful use of it all along the way, to our benefit, and to His glory. The reader will find the narratives related to some of these other adventures in the books we mentioned in the introduction to this book.

We will now continue and conclude this narrative portion with some glimpses into our story of leaving home to follow on the first steps of our call to seminary in Ambridge and the healing work that the Lord did in our first semester there.

7

❧

Our Spring and Summer Travelogue

No sooner had I begun to heal physically from my surgery than I also began to experience an intense urging from the Lord to proceed with the inner healing work that I, and, in reality, both of us, had already begun. Indeed, just two nights after my operation, our assistant rector made a hospital call and, to his astonishment, found me propped up in bed, eagerly devouring several books on the subject. He heartily approved of my efforts. But now, though I felt that I had already received a certain degree of emotional healing, I was starting to realize that I had barely begun this most challenging task. What follows is a chronological look at that ongoing healing journey in both of us, as taken from our journals from the time immediately following my surgery until our arrival at our little domicile in Ambridge.

<u>4-7-92</u>

By now, the reader has perhaps figured out that I can tend to be a little hard on, and a little impatient with, myself! On this particular evening, and only six days after my surgery, I complained to the Lord

71

about the blockages I was still feeling regarding my process of emotional healing! He responded with Mark 6:1-6, which tells the story of Jesus' visit to his hometown of Nazareth, and of the disbelief and rejection He encountered there. Verses 4 and 5 read: "Jesus said to them, 'Only in his hometown, among his relatives and in his own house is a prophet without honor. He could not do any miracles there, except lay his hands on a few sick people and heal them.'" (NIV)

The Lord was now beginning in earnest to indicate that we, too, would need to leave our home environment if we were to have a full and effective ministry. But I was also coming to see that only by leaving could I achieve any further degree of emotional healing, since every encounter with my parents served, not only to reopen old wounds but to add fresh ones. I was simply not strong enough to fight this battle on my old turf. The blissful hint in the midst of the Lord's word, so needed on the night before receiving my final biopsy report, was that I would indeed live.

4-10-92

Now, following the joyous news from that report, we could begin in earnest to focus on the path ahead. Allen wrote,

> "After praising the Lord, and acknowledging His hand in our lives, I prayed for guidance in our current situation. I wonder whether I'm showing a lack of trust by not being able to risk a little--by waiting for the absolutely certain word of guidance. I thought I just got the words, *'You can only steer a boat that is in motion under its own power.'* I then saw a cup, cut in half lengthwise--a cup that could not hold liquid."

The odd half-cup simply could not contain the blessing that the Lord, for His part, desired to pour out. It was our own fear that was causing us to negate those blessings by our hesitancy to step out in faith, albeit with faltering steps.

<u>4-11-92</u>

Allen wrote, "We prayed about our directions in life, saying, 'We are sick of listening to ourselves, Lord. Are You sick of listening to us?' to which I heard, *'Relax and let Me do it.'*" The Lord knew that we were utterly exhausted from our own striving, including our striving to understand. The only answer for us was to hand the controls over to Him.

Since we were, at this point, beginning to seriously consider Allen's possible call to seminary, he next wrote:

> "Jan then asked if I should go to seminary and seek
> ordination, and I saw a case or a box like a jewelry box,
> with an opened lid. The case seemed to have horizontal
> stripes of different colors, and a velvety interior which
> had light emanating from it."

This box symbolized to us the path about which we had just prayed. Intriguingly attractive, its interior played upon our natural curiosity, inviting closer inspection. "Come and look inside this lovely box," the Lord seemed to be coaxing, "and see what delightful things I have in store for you." Next, Allen was led to read Romans 12:2, a firm reminder of the means by which we were to understand God's will: "Do not conform any longer to the pattern of this world, but be transformed by the renewing of your mind. Then you will be able to test and approve what God's will is--his good, pleasing and perfect will." (NIV)

Since the scriptural prescription for the renewing of the mind centers on Bible study, fellowship, and prayer, the message with which the Lord followed made all the more sense. Allen continued,

> "As I prayed about our feelings of frustration--Jan's with
> where we are living, and mine with the car business, I

saw a row of bare trees or bushes with the branches all reaching upwards very intensely."

I sensed that these trees, with their bare branches stretching towards heaven, represented a group of believers who were earnestly praying for us. Was this image the Lord's way of telling us that the resolution of our vocational and other issues needed to include submitting them to the discernment of a praying body of fellow believers? Philippians 1:10 confirmed and expanded upon this: "...so that you may be able to discern what is best and may be pure and blameless until the day of Christ ..." (NIV)

These messages combined to state the same reality: As long as we clung to the world's way of thinking, and neglected to avail ourselves of the Body's discernment, our own discernment would be impaired, and our decision-making skewed. The Lord's closing words were, *"Read, write, teach,"* and *"Don't be afraid."*

4-12-92

Allen wrote:

> "I know that the Lord has promised good to me, but I act as though I don't believe it. I just keep trying to make things work out by main strength--by trying really hard to control everything--but I'm doing a very poor job. Sometimes I see myself as a bit pitiful, in the sense that I have clear talents and gifts, but I'm so conformed to the world that I'm afraid to use them. Our fear of financial loss prevents us from acting, even though we know that losing everything in God's service is far preferable to gaining everything and never using our gifts. It is very tempting to do the familiar things-- sort of like wearing old, dirty clothes that are not very becoming, but which I'm used to. God offers me the

chance to transform myself, but I must become naked and vulnerable, undressing before I can put on my new garments. I almost feel that if I don't change, I will surely die, at least inside. So, it comes down to some tough choices: admitting what a fool I've been for my persistence in these businesses that didn't use my abilities, and also, along with that, admitting my financial ineptitude. Then, there comes a choice which involves shaking some worldly foundations--losing control of those areas by which I order my secular life--and trusting in God for guidance in the darkness."

As I reread these words years later, I hasten to add that I do not believe the Lord is asking every business or sales person to quit what they are doing. In fact, those can and should be excellent avenues for the exercise of one's gifts, and for connecting with unbelievers. The issue is always God's call.

<u>4-16-92</u>
Allen wrote:

"I should describe the unusual dream I had last night. I was with a group of people in a city with a river running through it. I remember having to walk over a bridge to get to a university building. Then, Jan and I were with a group of people--some seemed to be from our church--and we were walking by a wide spillway that was right in the center of town, perpendicular to the main street, but somewhat under it. As I watched, I noticed large numbers of salmon in this spillway, and I decided to fish. However, it was mid-to-late afternoon, and there was no place to rent fishing equipment. Then someone found a couple of local people who lent us their equipment. I took a pole, and immediately noticed a school of fish, one of which was very large. I cast my line in front of this fish and, as it grabbed the hook, I reeled it in. When I had caught it, it seemed less large than it had in the water--a little disappointing--but I knew I could fish some more. However, at that moment, the water flow coming down the spillway was shut off, leaving only a dry channel. I, along with the others who were fishing, was disappointed, but I could see off in the distance a large and very blue lake, in full sunshine, as opposed to the late afternoon shadows where I was, where I thought I could continue fishing. Then I woke up."

What would later most strike me, upon arriving in Ambridge for the first time, was its remarkable resemblance to the town of this dream, for dominant in its scenery were the river and the bridge, just two blocks from our house! The university building quite likely represented the seminary, and fishing, Biblically speaking, always symbolizes evangelism, which was one of Trinity's main foci. However, there is also an intimation that the fishing would, at some point in the future, proceed at another and more promising location.

<u>4-19-92</u>

Allen wrote, "As I prayed for help in our decision-making, I received this scripture from 2 Corinthians 7:9: "...yet now I am happy, not because you were made sorry, but because your sorrow led you to repentance. For you became sorrowful as God intended and so were not harmed in any way by us." (NIV)

In the same way that Paul regretted those sins of the Corinthians that necessitated his letter, but did not regret the letter itself, so likewise the Lord regretted the necessity for my (Jan's) correction but was glad that it had produced the appropriate response of repentance in me. The net result was that my illness had not only left me unharmed but had been a means of great blessing. It is worth noting that sorrow, *in and of itself,* does not constitute repentance, but is rather the prelude to it. True repentance is evidenced by a changed life.

Allen continued, "Then, I saw a desk-top on which was a small electronic device that looked like a calculator with a funny strap. On the same desk-top there was also a white blotter, and printed on it was a large number 8." There it was again! I sensed that the calculator was the Lord's. Once more, He was saying that new beginnings were His intention for us. It was in His divine calculation that we would begin our new life, symbolized by the number 8, in the *eighth* month, August. The white blotter perhaps further described the Lord's ability, not only to forgive sin, but to heal the past, as well--a process that would also receive a new impetus with our August home leaving. This blotting-out will ultimately assume its eternal dimension, for in Isaiah 65:17, the Lord declared: "Behold, I will create new heavens and a new earth. The former things will not be remembered, nor will they come to mind." (NIV)

In the meantime, the Lord had another message concerning my emotional pain, as indicated by the next image of which Allen wrote: "I saw a foil package with six or so pills in it, which I knew to be a strong narcotic. The back of the package had been opened enough to reveal part of one or two of the pills, but not quite enough to take them out yet. I knew they were dangerous."

At the time, this image utterly baffled me, since taking narcotics has never had the slightest allure for either Allen or I, and I had already ceased to need any pain relief related to my surgery. It was only as a result of a later conversation with a friend that I suddenly understood the Lord's meaning. I believe He was addressing a tendency in the inner healing process to want to dull its pain, to deaden the sensibilities by emotionally blocking out the hurt of past experiences, and to avoid the difficult work of healing. I had already begun to peel back the foil on that package. Precisely the opposite response, however, was necessary if healing was to occur. The painful memories, shoved down for too long, had to come to the surface and brought into Christ's healing light. One specific area where I needed to allow this involved the emotions and fears surrounding my surgery. My friend suggested that, when writing about it, I should describe those scenes as vividly as possible, recalling my emotions as I did so. I trust I have adequately done that, for there is a mysterious way in which reliving an experience through the writing process brings healing. In that regard, I have recently found myself having periodic flashbacks related to particular episodes of childhood physical and emotional abuse from my mother. When we prayed about it, Allen heard the Lord say, *"Write her a letter."* I have been doing that, and recalling the incidents, while also letting her know that I love her and I forgive her. I have found that exercise helpful, both for me and surely for her, and I recommend it.

<u>4-20-92</u>
Allen wrote:

> "I feel an overwhelming sense that I don't have much time to make a major change. I don't know if it's the stress on me, or a window of opportunity being closed, but I feel that something bad--very bad--will happen if I can't act and can't trust. I am so bound by my fleshly self that I'm not sure that I *can* trust fully. I feel like I'm taking a step into thin air. Even though God has promised, it's still hard to believe that there will be something solid to step on. This inner urge is so strong that I have to fight just to keep doing what I'm doing. I wonder if everyone who is called in some strong way goes through these inner battles. Are some people better prepared by their past to trust that something good can happen if they don't control every minute of their lives?"

Having written these words, we turned to prayer concerning my relationship with my parents. For years, as I have related, I had deluded myself into thinking that I harbored no anger, resentment, or lack of forgiveness towards them. In actuality, nothing could have been farther from the truth, for despite my best efforts to suppress and deny the hurts, I had periodically exploded.

Now, a lifetime's worth of anger began to bubble unabated to the surface, with an intensity that surprised and shocked, not only me, but also Allen, who was often the recipient of my uncorked rage. For weeks I experienced an anger that frightened me and puzzled others, as the volcano was finally allowed to erupt. It would take months of inner healing work before these eruptions subsided and equilibrium was restored. In the meantime, I became increasingly alarmed at my own behavior and responses, but seemed unable to control myself. I was all the more distressed, since I had vowed after my surgery to be a new person. That blithe delusion had lasted for all of three weeks!

Yet the Lord often offers comfort and encouragement in unusual ways and in unexpected places. Thus, it was by no accident, I'm sure, that while reading C. S. Lewis' The Voyage of the Dawn Treader, I came upon these words: "It would be nice, and fairly nearly true, to say that 'from that time forth Eustace was a different boy. To be strictly accurate, he began to be a different boy. He had relapses. There were still many days when he could be very tiresome. But most of these I shall not notice. The cure had begun."

This describes the start of Eustace's transformation. How closely I identified! Like Eustace, I had begun to be different. Like Eustace, I too had relapses, and was no doubt frequently tiresome! And, like Eustace, my cure had begun.

Meanwhile, combined with my anger was a renewed sense of frustration with my life and vocation. Hence, at the start of prayer on this particular evening, I asked the Lord what I was doing with myself. *"You are my precious child,"* He rejoined. Once more, it seemed, *doing* took a back seat to *being*. Relationship was paramount.

Now, as I began to heal physically, I also began to face the prospect of the resumption of the weekly visits to my parents. However, I still did not have the emotional stamina to establish boundaries, nor even to extend the amount of time between visits. When I asked the Lord how I could visit without being hurt, Allen wrote: "I saw what looked like the dark edge of a planet with a fiery red light shining around it. The planet seemed to be blocking the force of the heat and flame on the other side." I felt that the Lord was telling me that He, as the planet, would shield me from the effects of any abuse I might encounter. Philippians 1:2-17 (NIV) was then given, with verses 6 and 12 being especially comforting: "...being confident of this, that he who began a good work in you will carry it on to completion until the day of Christ Jesus." And, "Now I want you to know, brothers, that what has happened to me has really served to advance the gospel."

4-21-92

"We asked for protection from negative thoughts and discouragement for Jan as she heals," wrote Allen. The Lord replied with his spiritual prescription of forgiveness, of putting on the new self, and of keeping my eyes fixed on Him, giving me Colossians 3:1-10. Most striking were verses 1 and 8: "Since, then, you have been raised with Christ, *set your hearts* on things above, where Christ is seated at the right hand of God. But now *you must rid yourselves* of all such things as these: *anger, rage*, malice, slander..." (NIV italics mine) The strong imperatives in these verses indicated that, although the healing work was the Lord's, I had a clear responsibility to take my own initiative in the process.

When I went on to ask the Lord again about the number 8 on the desk blotter, Allen heard, *"No regrets. Like Paul, run the race."* My tendency had always been not only to dwell on the past, but, even worse, to punish myself for past failures. "Don't look back," the Lord was urging. "I have given you a new beginning. Therefore, imitate Paul: press on to the goal ahead."

4-23-92

Allen wrote, "We keep asking the Lord about our vocations. We both feel lost and unable to really see our roles in the world. I see a step made of stone, but terribly cracked and loose." Here was a graphic image of our plight, for the step on which we were standing resembled the thinking and actions on which we had based our lives. Most specifically, it likely represented our current vocational situation. There was great urgency in getting off of this step before the Lord allowed it to crumble beneath us, sending us toppling to the ground.

4-25-92

On this evening, I had been anxiously seeking the Lord's guidance in preparation for the following day's visit to my parents, the first since my surgery. Allen wrote: "After I had shut out the lights, I saw an area with lots of small green islands, looking something like a swamp. Then I saw a small house, with two greenhouse-type windows sticking out from each front corner and wrapping around the corner to the side." The small house seemed to describe me, its greenhouse-style windows suggesting healthy, as well as health-giving breasts. Here, I felt, was a promise of healing in the areas related to nurturing, as well as an exhortation to *be* a nurturer. The two are inextricably connected, since it is in helping others that we are often healed. The meaning of the swamp, however, was something of a puzzle, and so we prayed about it again the next morning. Allen wrote, "Jan is asking again about the visit this afternoon with her parents, and about the heaviness she feels. I heard, *"It's a swamp, but I am the boat!"* Jan then asked about changing her responses, and needing help to do that, and the Lord said, *"'You have help. This is an opportunity. I will not leave you comfortless.'"* As I wrote this, I was reminded that so often in the Psalms, David likened his difficulties to being in a quagmire--a swamp."

4-28-92

On this date, as I prayed again about my parents, the scripture the Lord gave was 2 Corinthians 1:3-4. It reads, "Praise be to the God and Father of our Lord Jesus Christ, the Father of compassion and the God of all comfort, who comforts us in all our troubles, *so that we can comfort those* in any trouble with the comfort we ourselves have received from God." (NIV) I knew I was being exhorted to pass on to others in distress the comfort that I had received. No gift is ours merely to keep.

One month had now passed since my surgery. My physical healing was progressing remarkably well, but our financial and emotional lives were in turmoil. The prayer journey, of course, continued.

<u>5-1-92</u>

Allen wrote: "Jan asked for healing of her resentments in the situation with her parents. I saw a vision of a sheet of light or water coming down slowly, as if to cleanse all of that past life. Then, I saw the image of a book surrounded by light. I am sure it was the Bible, since I could see gold lettering on the front, of approximately the same size and number of letters as 'HOLY BIBLE.'" The Lord seemed to be saying, "Don't neglect My Word, for it is the ultimate authority concerning the healing of relationships."

Following these images came this marvelous promise from 2 Corinthians 1:10: "He has delivered us from such a deadly peril, and he will deliver us. On him we have set our hope that he will continue to deliver us ..." (NIV)

<u>5-4-92</u>

This was the date of my one-month post-surgical exam. Although there was no longer any reason whatsoever for me to be worried, this did not prevent me from nearly hyperventilating with fear! Despite all of the Lord's encouragement, it seemed that when under stress, my fear always overcame my trust. But the Lord consoled me with Ephesians 3:2: "Surely you have heard about the administration of God's grace that was given to me for you ..." (NIV)

During this time, my attention had also begun to turn to the writing I knew I was being called to do. I was anxious to be obedient, yet incapable of starting the task, like a car whose engine was revving, but whose gears were still disengaged! As I prayed about this, Allen saw the tip of a pen that was lying down. Typically, we have found that whenever the Lord shows us something that is lying down, He is admonishing us to pick it up and take some required action.

Related to and immediately following Allen's vision, he received another: "I keep seeing a rift in a long, shallow valley, and I get the impression of pressure or movement, as though both sides are pressing together and wanting to roll under in the middle, but are unable to." It was months before I grasped what the Lord was telling me here. He could not bring final closure to my healing until I had written about it, or had at least begun. This may be true for others as well, for I believe that something happens in the spiritual realm when we surrender to this discipline. In the same way, it was probably no accident that Allen's gift of prophecy came only a month after he began faithfully keeping his daily prayer journal. The very existence of Sacred Scripture attests to the fact that the Lord wanted his messages written down.

5-6-92

The month of May also found me involved in a number of inner healing sessions with my rector and another member of our healing team. As I prayed about my persistent anxieties, Allen heard the Lord say, *"Let it go. Trust in Me."* But oh! How I continued to struggle with this simple yet profound advice.

I also proceeded to pray about the continuing hope of a possible trip to Israel. As I did so, Allen reported seeing a map that was focused on the place where the Israelites had come out of Egypt as they headed toward the Promised Land. While this vision certainly had much spiritual import, on this occasion I appropriated it as a literal promise, as well!

5-8-92

Allen wrote, "Jan and I are in prayer this morning regarding several issues. Jan asked about her inner healing and about putting all of these things behind her, and I heard, *'You can't put them behind you. You must put them into My hands.'* Jan then asked about the spider image that our rector had been given yesterday when praying with her. (In his vision, he had seen a spider in a web, repeatedly lunging at and biting its victim in order to stun it.) I then heard the Lord say, *'"Don't be paralyzed by fear."'* This frightening image fit me all too well, for my dictionary defines *paralyze* as "to bring to a condition of helpless inactivity." The

Lord knew that fear in its many forms had indeed paralyzed me for years. His remedy was not complex, but rather took the form of a simple command predicated on trust.

5-10-92

Allen wrote, "The other evening, as I was lying in bed, quietly praying to the Lord for help in our material circumstances and in our directions, I saw the image of a woman's head, wearing a funny brown hat that looked like an oversized beret." The significance of the woman and her odd head covering intrigued but eluded me, but it would not be long before the Lord Himself would give us the interpretation of this enigmatic vision.

5-12-92

Allen wrote, "Last night I was in a very strange and quiet mood. I was sitting on the couch, with my eyes open, and I saw a window in the process of closing. I immediately thought, 'Is it a window of opportunity closing?'" Jan next asked about the woman with the beret, and I heard, *'The woman represents the cares of the world.'* We again prayed about the window, and my sense about it, and I heard, *'You saw correctly.'*" I knew that it was not a coincidence that these images had come so closely together, for it was precisely because we were so overburdened by the world's cares that the window was shutting on the opportunity for change. Incidentally, the image of the woman in the brown beret underscores the need for the Lord to be involved in interpretation. There are times when we can get a very partial sense of what the Lord seems to be saying--and that, only because, through the action of the Holy Spirit, He has allowed it. In the case of the woman, however, no amount of study, educated guessing, or speculation could have produced the interpretation that the Lord Himself gave.

5-14-92

Allen wrote, "This morning, as we were entering into prayer, I asked, 'Father God, what do you want me to do?' *'Use the gifts,'* He answered.

Jan then asked once more about the window that I had seen closing. John 3:10 was the Lord's stinging and yet humorous response: "'You are Israel's teacher,' said Jesus, 'and do you not understand these things?'" (NIV) As the reader has, perhaps, already noticed, I often persisted in praying about something long after I should have gotten the message! "I may be dense," I protested to the Lord, "but at least I persevere!"

Meanwhile, we had made one positive move towards change. Back in March, while I was away on my fasting retreat, Allen had taken the tentative step of filling out and mailing an application to seminary. The plan was to get a one-year degree in Missions and Evangelism from Trinity Episcopal School for Ministry in Ambridge, Pennsylvania, and then return home, better equipped to do ministry there. Now, he wrote, "Jan prayed about how we could break out of our confusion into purposeful action. As she asked about Trinity, I heard, *'You must obey,'* just as a very strong stream of sunlight came into the room. Jan next asked about her inner healing process. *'Let the light in,'* I heard."

I had been locked in a prison of self-inflicted bondage for so long that I scarcely knew how to begin to follow this imperative. Yet this conjunction of words and image reinforced once again that leaving was not only about vocation and calling, but also healing. We were to begin a new life and ministry together in a place apart. Indeed, a member of our healing team at church received a startling confirmation of this one Sunday when I went forward for prayer. As she prayed, she had a vision of Allen and me, standing before the altar, as though being married again. This image instantly recalled and confirmed my own campground dream of several weeks before. As if to reinforce this theme, our rector prayed for me during this same period, and received Ruth Chapter 2. There Ruth leaves her father and mother and home and goes to work in the fields of Boaz, her kinsman-redeemer.

5-19-92

On this date I (Jan) recorded this fascinating entry in my own journal:

"Last night I had an interesting dream, and one pertinent to my inner healing struggles. In the first part, I was being pursued by a man who was trying to kill me. We were in a large building that seemed a bit like a hotel. I fled in fear, and ran from the building out into an area that seemed to be on the outskirts of a gloomy city. Fatigued from running on foot, I decided to go back and get my car. I found it parked in an isolated area, a Peugeot with metallic blue paint. As I approached the car, I was aware that there was a woman inside. Her presence was startling, bizarre, and somewhat threatening. She was in the back seat, facing the rear window, and was clawing and pulling at the upholstery with her hands. When I asked her what she was doing in my car, she replied, 'You have an oil leak, and I'm helping you fix it.' I recall thinking that I had no knowledge that there was anything wrong with the car. Besides this, she was shredding the inside of the back seat, not fixing any oil leak. Yet, as I looked at the ground near the car, I saw a splatter of what appeared to be like oil or blood, but not quite either. I was then relieved to find that the woman had gotten out of the car, but almost immediately she was back inside, having gone around to the other door. Next, I was aware of a man standing beside the car. He was blond, and clearly seemed to be the woman's husband. The woman began speaking to him. Her speech was incoherent, but he seemed not to recognize its insanity. Then, I was at the rear of the car, and the trunk was open. The man and woman were lying inside it, curled up in fetal positions next to each other. At this point, the woman gave the appearance of drunkenness. I shouted in anger at the man, saying, 'She's flat-out drunk, and it's time that somebody told you.' Seeming to be confronted with the truth for the first time, he broke down and began to sob. At that, I woke up."

The couple lying in the car represented my parents, I believe, and their fetal positions indicated to me that their behaviors arose from their own unresolved childhood issues and fears. Furthermore, their actions in the dream illustrated quite dramatically the dysfunction I have earlier described. When I related the dream to my pastor, he affirmed that it was Christ who was my Pursuer, and that His intent had been to bring, not destruction, but repentance, healing, and amendment of life. I was being called to die to myself.

5-20-92

Allen wrote, "I am in a terrible, black mood this morning, as Jan and I are sitting in the living room. I can't pray, but Jan is praying. As she began, I received 1 Corinthians 2:9: 'However, as it is written: No eye has seen, no ear has heard, no mind has conceived what God has prepared for those who love him.'(NIV) Next, I saw a web being pulled apart from the top of my vision down. Jan then prayed, 'Lord, we're not even sure if our business difficulties are being caused by You, by Satan, or by our own ineptitude.' I heard, *It's Me!*"

This spoke to us of three things. First, the Lord was comforting us with a reminder of the blessings He had in store for us, both now and in eternity. Second, He was showing us that, despite the way things might have appeared to us at the time, Satan's plans to ensnare and defeat us were already being unraveled. We were not to despair. Third, God was providing confirmation that it was He Himself who was orchestrating our troubles in order to cause us to change!

5-24-92

Allen wrote, "Jan prayed about her parents, her frustration and sense of bondage, and about what she should do. I saw a door with a thick wooden bar across it, but it was standing by itself, with no frame, or even walls. Jan continued to pray about the situation, and I heard, *Who are you serving?*" As an emotional prisoner of my own making, I was battering against this barred door, when all around it stood freedom. The Lord's pointed query to me elicited painful reflection. Who *was* I serving? I had to admit that I really wasn't sure, but, given His question, chances were pretty good it wasn't always Him! On that topic, we have enjoyed Father Dave Pivonka's superb film on the life of Saint Francis of Assisi, entitled *Sign of Contradiction*. One of the early and critical turning points comes for Francis when, in the midst of his great anguish over which course to pursue in life--knighthood or the Lord's work--he clearly hears the Lord ask him, "Who is it better to serve--the master or the servant?" Francis readily concludes that it is the master, though his motives were not yet fully converted.

<u>5-26-92</u>

Allen wrote, "We are praying about our roles, our destiny, and our finances, and I heard the words, *'You need to pray with others.'*" The Lord knew we were still neglecting to commit our concerns on a regular basis to a larger group of discerning believers. Then came the scripture Jeremiah 10:17: "Gather up your belongings to leave the land, you who live under siege."(NIV) Once again, we were being treated to the Lord's droll sense of humor. What was *not* quite so funny was that we still weren't fully getting the message!

<u>5-28-92</u>

This dullness on our parts sometimes occasioned a harsher word from the Lord. On this particular date, our questions about our callings brought this response: *"When the master comes..."* The scriptural allusions were clear. In parable after parable, Jesus sternly warned that He expected to find His servants about His work when He returned. Those who were not so occupied, He declared, were not His true servants, and would be excluded from the Kingdom. (See, for example, Matt. 24:45-51, and 25:14-30).

<u>6-1-92</u>

The following month began with some eminently practical advice: "Tonight, Jan and I are praying together for guidance and understanding," Allen wrote. "We confessed our uncertainty and our desire to obey, adding that we weren't fully sure what to do. I saw a huge eagle with enormous wings spread wide, though it was not flying, but perched. It seemed both alive and made of a golden color." This bold image immediately struck me as being a pictorial representation of Isaiah

40:31: "but those who hope in the Lord will renew their strength. *They will soar on wings like eagles.....*" (NIV italics mine) Like the Babylonian exiles, we were weary from our captivity, and yet, poised like the eagle, we awaited with eager expectation the clear word from the Lord that would refresh us and release us on our flight. Finally, "We asked the Lord if He had anything else to call to our attention, and I heard, *'Take more quiet time.'*"

<u>6-4-92</u>

Allen wrote, "Last night, as Jan was asking the Lord about our frustration regarding direction, I heard the question, *'Who's in charge?'*" Obviously, we *weren't*, but our behavior indicated that we often thought we were. After all, isn't that the place from which we fallen humans erroneously derive our security? This was to be but one of many instances when the Lord would challenge us with that very same question: *"Who's in charge?"* Allen continued, "As I was praying about trusting, and how difficult it is to trust with the world's worries upon us, I felt a sense of intense dizziness while my eyes were closed, but which went away as soon as I opened them." This dizziness indicated that we needed, were being advised of, and were about to experience a spiritual shaking-up. Revelation 2:4 followed: "Yet I hold this against you: You have forsaken your first love.'" (NIV) The words stung, forcing me to serious self-examination. I recalled our heart-felt love for the Lord when we had first gone back to church some years earlier, and I realized that we had gradually and almost imperceptibly begun falling away from that zealous and simple devotion. Who or what had stolen our hearts? The prime suspect was the woman in the brown beret!

<u>6-8-92</u>

Allen wrote, "Jan asked about her writing and about feeling blocked. I heard, *'You need a deadline.'* Jan asked how she was to get this deadline. I then heard, *'You know how to get a deadline.'*" "But, Lord," I whined, "I *don't* know." The only time in my life when I had ever had an externally imposed writing deadline was in *school.* "Lord," I began to wonder, "is *that* how I am supposed to get a deadline?" If I had been able to see His Face, I suppose that He might have been grinning. One can see, I might add, that the Lord does not think much of our excuses!

In the meantime, I continued to have days when I was filled with anger and frustration, often directed at myself and at my own inability to change and, as time went on, I became increasingly frightened and anxious. To make matters worse, the renewed visits to my parents were invariably resulting in frustration and exasperation. Consequently, prayer sessions like the following one were typical of this period.

<u>6-15-92</u>

"Jan and I are praying together this morning," Allen wrote. "Jan prayed about the situation with her parents, and the mess that their house is in." The Lord counseled with Matthew 10:14: 'If anyone will not welcome you or listen to your words, *shake the dust off your feet* when you leave that home or town.'" (NIV, italics mine)

I laughed out loud, for one of my continuing sources of irritation had been my father's utter neglect of all household chores. My mother had now been in a nursing home for two and a half years, and Allen and I had been the only ones doing all of the cleaning and laundry. We might have paid to have some help come in, but he would never have tolerated it. The Lord told us that the chaos was largely deliberate on my father's part--a means of expressing his anger and resentment at me for what he saw as my abandonment of *him*. Needless to say, we couldn't even begin to keep up with all the work, and the house increasingly re-flected my father's spirit of confusion and depression. The curtains were yellowed and stiff from nicotine, mounds of dust collected under the beds, despite my efforts to keep them under control, and dirty dishes stayed in the sink from visit to visit. In addition, large quantities of paperwork and mail began to amass in numerous haphazard piles. Con-sequently, now added to our list of regular chores was the endless task of sorting through it all, but somehow we never managed to complete the job before more of the stuff appeared. Incredibly, however, though he was in the early stages of Alzheimer's, my father drove his car every day without incident, took himself out for meals, visited my mother at the nursing home twice a day, and somehow managed to pay every bill on time! Hence, it certainly did seem that much of the mess was a statement directed at me and at us.

Meanwhile, if my father was angry and depressed, so was I. I was torn by conflicting emotions. First, the *child* in me wanted to keep the house as my mother had cared for it, and as I had remembered it in better times. She had always been an artful and meticulous housekeeper. Second, the *daughter* in me simply could not bear to see my own father living in the midst of such dirt and clutter, while he, on the other hand, almost seemed to enjoy it, which only made me more irritated. Finally, the healing *adult* in me knew that the only option that really made sense was to be obedient to the scripture verse, and to leave the "dust" behind. However, the verse also had more serious import, for when I asked further about it, the Lord added, *"You have no honor in your own country,"* a reference to Mark 6:4.

Our prayer dialogue continued. Allen wrote, "Jan is filled with anger and frustration, and she asked the Lord if we needed to physically move away. I heard, *'Be obedient to Me,'* and then *'There is always a choice,'* followed by, *'I adjure you to come close to Me.'*" Now, *adjure* is a strong word. It means, first: to charge, bind, or command, earnestly and solemnly, often under oath or the threat of a curse, and second: to entreat or request earnestly. I sensed that I was in deep spiritual and emotional trouble. Allen wrote, "Jan then prayed for inner healing, and I heard, *'Soak yourself in Me.'*" When she asked *how* she was to come close to God, and to soak herself, I heard, *'You must see the wonder in all of it.'* Wow! I paused and read over that last word several times, trying to take it into my heart and spirit. If the Lord had never spoken another word to us that word alone would have sufficed. *"You must see the wonder in all of it."*

Allen continued, "Jan next prayed about the frequency of visiting her parents, and her attitude towards it, and I saw a large crab claw coming up from below." The claw aptly symbolized to me the grasping, controlling behavior I was being subjected to during my visits home. In hindsight, I would add that my parents themselves were probably largely unaware of the effect of their behaviors, but were rather acting out of their own pain and their own subconscious fears.

Later that night, as we resumed our prayer, Allen further wrote, "Jan is asking for guidance in the situation with her parents, and asking that she not be chastised further. I heard, *'I am a God of love.'*" Clearly, what was perhaps my most difficult inner healing issue, and likely the central one, was finally being allowed to show itself for what it was. Subjected by my mother to a lifetime of criticism and misplaced punishment, I had unknowingly projected these attributes onto the Lord. I had come to see Him as a harsh judge who was waiting only to find fault and to punish. Worse yet, I had become convinced that He would deal severely with me for these emotions that I was desperately struggling to control. In response, the Lord comforted and encouraged me with Ephesians 2:10: "For we are God's workmanship, created in Christ Jesus to do good works, which God prepared in advance for us to do."(NIV) The Lord was reassuring me that, in the midst of it all, He had a sovereign plan for my life. If I continued to walk by faith, following the path, He would work His will through me.

6-16-92

Allen wrote, "It is just after supper, and Jan and I are praying especially about Jan's call to vocation. As she prayed, I heard the Lord say, *'I have given you great blessings.'* Then, I saw something that looked like a cocoon, but it was wriggling! Last, I saw a spider's web, but it had a wedge cut out of it."

I saw that I was the transformed caterpillar, struggling to emerge as a lovely butterfly, and the thought was both comical and comforting. The image of the web was very like the one seen a month before. Easily discouraged, I needed repeated reminders that Satan's net of entrapment and destruction was already being dismantled.

In these exchanges, I was richly blessed by the Lord's expressions of love for me and by His gentle exhortations. But, like any good parent, He also needed to show His tougher side. Thus, over the course of the next few days, our prayer would result in a rapid-fire series of surprisingly clear, pointed, and insistent responses from the Lord concerning our path and my emotional state.

<u>6-17-92</u>

Despite the good message from the day before, I was still anxious. I continued to pray about the emotions engendered by the visits to my parents, asking the Lord again if we needed to physically distance ourselves. Finally, in His own godly exasperation perhaps, the Lord bluntly advised, *"Go away."* That may well be about as direct as He has ever been with me. Then, reported Allen, "I saw three rings, and a line of light made with something like a bullet creating an arc through them. Next, this image turned into the letter 'omega,' the last letter in the Greek alphabet. Here was a happy reassurance. The three rings, I believe, were my mother, my father, and I. We would be together again, *in Christ, for all eternity.* After all, Jesus had said of Himself in Revelation 22:13, "I am the Alpha and *the Omega*, the First and *the Last*, the Beginning and *the End.*" (NIV, italics mine) For the present, the Lord seemed to be saying that it was both good and necessary that I be separated from my parents and, indeed, that the three of us be separated from each other. My mother would live in the nursing home, my father would continue in his house, and Allen and I would journey to Ambridge, Pennsylvania, and beyond.

<u>6-18-92</u>

Allen wrote, "As we started to pray tonight, I saw an umbrella-shaped object that seemed to be organic and moving--a kind of covering. Then I heard the word *'Columbus'* and saw a pair of scissors with the blades open. When Jan asked if these things related to us personally, I saw a motor, as on an airplane wing, with a double-bladed propeller which was at first still and then began spinning fairly rapidly." The organic, living umbrella, we thought, was the Lord Himself, assuring us that we were under His protection. And being thus covered, we would then be cut free to sail forth, like Columbus, on a great adventure. The spinning propeller reinforced the message: we were about to take off!

Allen continued, "Jan then asked about her anger issues, and I heard, *'Is it righteous anger or selfish anger?'*" This piercing and unexpected question hit me hard and, after some painful reflection, I was forced to admit that not all of my anger was righteous. Though I was fearful, the question also prodded me to inquire further. Allen next wrote, "Jan asked about her inner healing, wondering if she had 'severed the umbilical cord,' and how she would know when she had. I heard the word *'approval,'* followed by, *'I am all the approval you need.'*"

These words also struck home for I realized that what still bound me was my subconscious dependence upon my parents' permission, praise, sanction, and favor. I would know that I was truly free when I had fully transferred these emotional needs to the Lord. Again Allen wrote, "As we then prayed about Jan's needing the Lord's help with these things, He rejoined, *'You need others.'* Immediately, I saw a group of three or four old-fashioned milk bottles--glass, with cardboard tops." The milk bottles conveyed a sense of nurturing from others, particularly perhaps from older women who could provide healthy mothering. However, the following word, *"You must forget yourself,"* provided balance and a reminder that I was also to help and nurture *others*. I knew that I had often been remiss in that regard.

6-19-92

On this evening, my anger, our financial stress, and our general frustration levels had combined to produce a heated argument between Allen and me. When our emotions were utterly spent, we finally sat down to do what we should have done in the first place--pray! Here are the results.

Allen wrote, "Jan and I are praying tonight for guidance and for inner healing for both of us. We are stressed by the world and its demands, and by our lack of performance. I heard, *'Do not fight, only trust.'*" We had not mentioned the fight as we began to pray, and yet this was the first subject that the Lord addressed. In the heat of the argument, we had forgotten that He was, of course, listening to the whole thing! Chagrined, we saw our concerns to be selfish and misguided.

It was so like the Lord to gently confront us about relationship issues before going on to listen and respond to our prayer concerns.

Allen then wrote, "Jan asked for healing of body, mind, and spirit, and I heard, *'It shall be.'*" However, he also received this sobering verse from Hebrews 3:11(NIV), which reads, "So I declared on oath in my anger, 'They shall never enter my rest.'" Provoked by our lack of faith, the Lord was warning us, as He had warned Israel in the wilderness, that our persistent insecurity regarding His provision and protection, in the face of all the evidence of His past blessing, would result in our loss of inner peace. The rebuke stunned me, but I continued to pray. Allen wrote, "Jan asked about the scissors that I had seen last night. *'They are Mine,'* said the Lord." These confirming words had a somber tone that reached beyond mere ownership to a fierce possessiveness. The Lord was in absolute control of these scissors, and would use them when and how He pleased. I had instinctively known that these scissors would have a further function, and I now understood that the Lord was also in the process of cutting us both loose from our bondage to our old lives.

His gracious advice was also offered, for the Lord's next words were, *"Don't be overburdened. My yoke is light."* Then He exclaimed, *"Can you not see? Have you not heard?"* Still frightened by the verse from Hebrews, I asked the Lord if He were angry with me. He answered, *"Only trust. I am your Light."* Nonetheless, I remained shaken, not only by the Lord's strong words, but, by my own runaway emotions. Given my recent surgery, and all of the physical, hormonal, and emotional changes that had rapidly ensued, I suppose that I might simply have rationalized my feelings and reactions, never seeing them as a signal of a need for deep change. Thankfully, I did not do so, for I was aware that I was still accountable before the Lord for my behaviors and responses. He knew I was struggling, but He also knew that I was capable of change, with His help.

Nonetheless, when we resumed our prayer later that evening, Allen wrote, "Jan and I are praying again at bedtime, since Jan is extremely fearful and frantic. She is afraid that her emotions, which she can't control, will bring judgment upon her. I said that God knows how hard it is for us to trust, and He keeps trying to correct our course." Increasingly anxious and afraid, however, I had begun to cry uncontrollably, but this only worsened my distress. It was not until later that I gained an insight into my odd reactions to my own tearful expressions of emotion. I recalled that throughout my childhood, my mother would herself become anxious and upset when I cried, and she would often say, "Stop crying. You'll make yourself sick." No wonder I had learned to suppress my feelings, especially of sorrow or grief! The reality was that stifling my natural emotional responses was far more likely to make me sick than crying was. I realize now that it would have been helpful to have had another kindly adult with whom I could talk, but that was not my situation. Now, the anger and tears of a lifetime were welling up and overflowing, but the old internal message was still there: if I released my emotions, I would distress others and make myself ill, as well.

Meanwhile, Allen wrote, "As we prayed about these issues, and about the situation with Jan's parents, I received these verses: "Now I want you to know, brothers, that what has happened to me has really served to advance the gospel. As a result, it has become clear throughout the whole palace guard and to everyone else that I am in chains for Christ." (Philippians 1:12-13)

These words of Paul again reminded me that *my* suffering also had a purpose: my testimony to the Lord's faithfulness would help to spread the good news of the Gospel. Satan's plan had been that my bondage would destroy me but, instead, my deliverance would serve to glorify the Lord and advance His kingdom.

The prayer about my parents continued, and Allen wrote, "I heard the words *'You must stay away.'* Then, I saw what looked like two narrow cliffs separated by a distance." The Lord's words were not a suggestion, but a command. For the sake of my physical, emotional, and spiritual wellbeing, it was imperative that I leave. I had to draw apart from family and my past, and distance myself from them, in order to begin in earnest the life and ministry to which the Lord was calling me, and us.

More disturbing was the next vision. Allen wrote, "After this, I saw an old woman with white hair and a flowered dress, in a sitting position. She seemed normal except that she had six arms." The image was too frightening to be simply funny, for this woman, I knew, was my mother, to whose manipulative and controlling behavior I had been subjected for so long. Even worse, the vision bore an undeniable resemblance to the Hindu goddess Shiva, whose title was "The Destroyer." The message was obvious. Finally, asking how I could honor my parents if I were to stay away, the Lord explained, *"To honor does not mean to submit."*

6-28-92

Allen wrote, "As we were praying about inner healing for both of us from childhood situations, I saw a row of harrow blades." I made another trip to the dictionary. A *harrow,* of course, is an agricultural implement designed to break up clods of soil before planting seed, and hence the image could allude to preparation for evangelism. As a verb, however, the word also means, "to disturb keenly or painfully; to distress the mind, feelings, etc." Thus, it was not surprising that immediately following the image of the harrow blades came these words of Israel's King Hezekiah, with the first of which I began my hysterectomy account, and which echo so well my own story of illness and recovery: "But what can I say? He has spoken to me, and he himself has done this. I will walk humbly all my years because of this anguish of my soul. Lord, by such things men live; and my spirit finds life in them too. You restored me to health and let me live. *Surely it was for my benefit that I suffered such anguish.* In your love you kept me from the pit of destruction you have put all my sins behind your back." (Isaiah 38:10-17, NIV) (italics mine)

With these verses, I was reminded again of the intimate connections between physical, emotional, and spiritual healing, for the soil of our souls required harrowing in order that the seeds of healing and change might be sown. I further saw that affliction--contrary to the modern worldview--is often a blessing the Lord allows for our correction and our perfecting.

Ultimately, my thoughts centered on the relationship of my

experience to that of all other believers, past, present, and future. Each of us has been called in various ways throughout our lives to repeat the journey of the Israelites. We must come out of the spiritual bondage of Egypt, and endure a time of testing in the wilderness, before we can fully enter into the Promised Land of our spiritual inheritance in Christ. As the writer of Hebrews declared in 4:9(NIV), "There remains, then, a Sabbath-rest for the people of God." Little did I know that our ongoing struggle would be to enter into that rest. Our prayer time the very next night served to underscore this point.

6-29-92

The closing days of the month of June brought with them the decision to follow up Allen's application to Trinity by traveling to Ambridge, Pennsylvania in order to visit the school and be interviewed. We had missed the annual Visitors' Weekend in March due to my nutritional retreat and impending surgery, but I was now beginning, for the first time after the operation, to feel that I had the stamina to make the eleven-hour drive each way. However, we were still mired in our old ways of thinking. Allen wrote, "Jan and I are praying together tonight just before we leave early tomorrow morning to go to Trinity. Jan was asking about money issues, and our feeling of incompetence regarding earning a living. I saw a triangle of fire with strange demon shapes and clutching tendrils." This startling image told us that we were still in serious spiritual danger, for despite all of the previous warnings and exhortations, we remained in the world's material grip.

When I went on to ask for the Lord's help in breaking our bondage to the world and trusting in Him, Allen heard, *Soon enough.* The words had a vaguely ominous ring and, indeed, before long, we would begin to discover that the Lord had devised ways of answering this prayer that we had neither imagined nor desired! But has He not said that our ways are not His ways?

On the last day of the month, we set off on our journey. My chief memory of the trip, other than its wearying length, and the soreness of my abdomen, was of the purple vetch that lined the sides of the highways across the entire width of Pennsylvania. In full bloom, and bathed in brilliant summer sunshine, the vetch seemed to be laid out as a royal carpet ushering us towards our destination. The next morning, we awoke refreshed, and strolled over to the seminary to begin the rest of our lives.

<u>7-1-92</u>

Allen wrote, "We are in Ambridge tonight as we investigate the possibility of going to Trinity. I had several tests this morning, and both of us were interviewed this afternoon. We will find out the results tomorrow. If accepted, we must then decide if this is truly the option that God has in mind for us."

In retrospect, it is amazing to me that we remained so continually blind and befuddled, so slow at discerning God's plan. And yet, paradoxically, we had a strange sense that the moment had not quite come for the veil of our confusion to be lifted. In the meantime, all we could do was persist in prayer.

Allen continued, "We asked for guidance and wisdom in this difficult process of searching. I then saw what looked like various pieces of loose white string, and heard, *'Keep following the path.'*" The strings confirmed and illustrated the paradox: while we were still "at loose ends," our indeterminate status seemed to be at least partially by God's design. His advice was simply to accept this temporary uncertainty and follow the path, one step at a time.

Allen next wrote, "Jan asked about *her* path and her need to have something meaningful to do, and I saw various things with wings: a bird, and several planes. As Jan then prayed that we be led to places and ministries that use our talents, I heard the word *'Areopagitica.'*" The wings clearly suggested flight, departure, migration, travel, and a change of location, not to mention an uplifting and a soaring of the spirit. Once again, meaningful activity for me was predicated on being in a new spiritual, physical, and emotional setting. The word *"Areopagitica"* was a bit more challenging, and remained unclear for a time, but from past English classes, I did seem to recall the word to be the title of a work by John Milton. Months later, when I thought to look it up, my recollection was confirmed: *"Areopagitica"* was the title of an essay by Milton championing freedom of the press and the right to publish. Here was an intriguing intimation. I would gradually come to see that my task, facilitated by my new environment, would be to write, and (dare I think?), to eventually publish. The interconnections were even subtler, since "aero" (with the *e* and the *r* reversed) is a Greek root pertaining to aircraft and flight! What's more, I had tried to begin the writing process while still at home but, lacking an academic environment and the encouragement of editors and other writers, my efforts had never really "gotten off the ground!" Now it would become increasingly obvious that we had *already* been led to that place and those ministries where we would begin to find our mission and use our talents.

7-2-92

We stopped in at Trinity to see if Allen had been accepted and, of course, he had. The acceptance, however, left us bemused. After all, a rejection would have been an easy "that's that," an affirmation that we could go back to the familiarity of our old lives, miserable as they had become, and forget about this whole scary adventure. But there was also the swelling sense of excitement, the tingling anticipation of an utterly new and fulfilling life in the offing. Now we had much praying to do, and several hard decisions to make. We were locked in an interior battle between the familiar and the unknown--and time was running out.

7-3-92

Allen wrote, "We have decided to stay in Ambridge until tomorrow so that we can talk to a few more people. We are terribly confused, especially since we found out today that we would have to be here on August 17th for orientation! That just seems impossible, given all that needs to be done."

As the realities of the impending changes began to assert themselves, we panicked, and half-managed to convince ourselves that perhaps none of this had been the Lord's plan, after all! Allen wrote, "As we were considering our feeling that perhaps the Lord is saying this isn't right, I heard, *'Think about community.'* Then, as Jan talked about her situation at home, and her need to change it, I heard (again), *'You need a deadline.'"*

Seeing that we were contemplating bailing out of the whole enterprise, the Lord made one final appeal based, not on academics, but on relationships. The bait was tempting, since we had regularly complained of a need for more friends and for greater involvement in Christian community. Now, and not by coincidence, the theme of a deadline had reappeared. Previously applied to my writing, the term now expanded to encompass our entire life-change! Without a specific schedule, and an immediate deadline, would we ever have had the impetus to make the move? The Lord knew that without this externally enforced discipline, we would likely have floundered in confusion indefinitely.

On the Fourth of July, we drove home, more filled with questions than answers. If we decided to go to school, how could we possibly get the house packed up? There were thousands of things to be done and a million details to attend to! Besides, I was still unable to do any lifting, or even engage in much strenuous activity, at all. Then, should we put the house up for sale? What if it didn't sell? How could we survive financially, with no income, and with expenses ticking away like a time bomb back at home? If the house did sell, would we ever be able to own another one? Was this whole seminary idea merely the self-indulgent fantasy of two disillusioned Baby Boomers? How could we say good-bye to church, family, and friends--and what about my parents?

There was one consolation. Allen had initially applied for the one-year degree program in Missions and Evangelism, since our assumption was that we might be returning in a year. Thus, the experience would be an interesting and challenging interlude, providing an exciting chance to grow and learn, after which we would come back equipped with new attitudes and skills. This assumption was likely a divinely inspired delusion, since the Lord knew that we could not have coped with a fuller understanding of His plan.

7-5-92

Allen wrote, "Jan said to the Lord that she didn't know if we'd be physically able to be out of here in six weeks. I again heard, *'You're not in charge.'*" By now, one would have thought we had figured that out! But the Lord's words, while pointedly humorous, gave us a fresh reminder that our inadequacies were irrelevant. Though we did not understand how, we nonetheless were being exhorted to trust that everything would somehow get done.

As I look back, I do not recall a specific point at which we made the firm decision to leave. Rather, each day nudged us closer to that reality. In concrete terms, this meant that we began to spend some time each day sorting through our household goods. We also began to talk and pray through the options concerning the sale or rental of the house. True to form, we also had frequent moments when doubts arose and dominated our thinking, and our prayer times reflected our perplexity.

7-6-92

Wrote Allen, "I have begun my fast as of last night, and we are praying this morning for guidance. I heard, *'The answer is in the Book.'*" Then, as Jan asked whether we should tell people about our house being for sale, the Lord said, *'Wait on Me.'*"

The Lord's first reply had a hint of rebuke for, all too often, we had sought wisdom that was contained in scripture if we would but read and meditate on it. The second reply was directed at our persistent impatience. Waiting was agonizing, but it was a discipline that we sorely needed to acquire. In retrospect, we have often realized that the immediate granting of our requests would have short-circuited both development of character and the learning of valuable spiritual lessons.

That evening Allen continued: "We are praying tonight, trying to discern what this call process is all about. Jan said that the discerning process is certainly difficult, and I immediately heard, *'It's not difficult,'* and then, *'Trust and explore.'* Next, Jan asked just what it was that we were supposed to be doing, and I heard, *'Don't be so obsessed with doing.*

What you become will shape what you do.'" I was to ponder these last words for a long time, for behind them lay a profound principle, the richness and depth of which would continue to unfold.

<u>7-7-92</u>

Allen wrote, "Jan asked the Lord if we are trying to make something happen that is not yet ready to happen. I heard, *'You are seeking My will.'* I then asked about the way in which we were being guided--meaning, to what degree was our *own* initiative to be a part of the process? Do we lift up anchor on our own ship, or do we wait for God's clear call to raise the anchor? I heard, *'You must do what you must do.'* Jan then asked why we always seemed to be going backwards financially where we were, and I heard, *'You must do what you must do.'* Then, *'I do guide through circumstances.'"*

What we had clearly begun to suspect was now being confirmed: it was the Lord who was, and who had been, engineering our discomfort. However, that same evening's prayer time showed that we still hadn't fully grasped the message. We may have been dense, but at least we were persistent! Allen wrote,

> "Night has fallen, and Jan and I are continuing to seek
> the Lord's will in this matter of seminary and selling the
> house, as well as in the other changes that those imply.
> I am feeling particularly stressed about the car business
> tonight, and I just don't understand why it should be
> so difficult at the moment. I feel like I can't even begin
> to meet my obligations, but perhaps that's part of God's
> plan. If things were going well financially, we might
> be tempted to stay, and not change anything. Yet Jan's
> operation and healing have made us acutely aware of
> just how fragile life is. And we are accountable to God
> for the talents He has given us in trust, as well. I cannot
> imagine giving an accounting to Christ right now for
> the meager things that I have done with those talents.

Praise God that He gives us many chances, though I'm convinced that when we won't listen, He taps us on the shoulder harder and harder. I think He is trying to warn us right now, as well as to break us of the material bondage in our lives, so that we can fully live for the first time."

As we entered again into prayer, my thoughts centered on my mother and father. Even after making the tentative decision to leave, I continued to have doubts as to whether it was indeed biblically sound for me to move away from my two ailing parents. When we asked the Lord about this, Allen wrote: "I saw an image of a suitcase standing upright, but it seemed to be sewn closed with heavy black thread." The Lord seemed to be saying, "It's a shut case. You have made up your mind to go. Don't change it now." My mental suitcase was laced closed, and I was not to *unpack* it again. Once more the Lord also reminded us of Genesis 13, the story of Lot's physical separation from Abraham.

Finally, our attention turned to the matter of the house: "Jan asked if we should put the house up for sale as a fleece, a test. As she did so, I got a sense of a caricature of a desert with a person moving across it, and with one cactus visible." I assumed at the time that my test was a perfectly reasonable means of determining the validity of our plans. After all, if the house did sell, wouldn't that be a clear affirmation of our call? If the house did not sell, was that not a sign that we really weren't supposed to leave? My little test was, of course, simply a thinly disguised means of putting ourselves back in control, but the cartoon-like desert image showed that the Lord hadn't been fooled in the slightest. And, though we failed to recognize it at the time, His seemingly oblique response had assured us that we were in for another wilderness experience! As proof, consider these words given us from Deuteronomy 8:2-5: "Remember how the Lord your God led you all the way in the *desert* these forty years, to humble you and to test you in order to know what was in your heart, whether or not you would keep his commands.

He humbled you, causing you to hunger and then feeding you with manna, which neither you nor your fathers had known, to teach you that *man does not live on bread alone but on every word that comes from the mouth of the Lord.* Your clothes did not wear out and your feet did not swell during these forty years. Know then in your heart that as a man disciplines his son, so the Lord your God disciplines you."(NIV)

Like the Israelites, we were obsessively focused on our material possessions, while the Lord sought instead to possess our hearts. We needed to be reminded that it was not as though the Lord Himself could not identify with our dilemma, for Jesus had quoted from this very passage during His own temptation in the wilderness (See Matthew 4:4). Now, in ways that we could not begin to fathom, we were about to be disciplined, humbled, and blessed, and it was *we* who would be tested.

7-9-92

As might be expected, however, the issue of the house weighed more heavily on us with each passing day. Aside from the erroneous idea of using the sale as a fleece, there was still the reality, it seemed to us, that the house needed to either be rented or put on the market, since leaving it empty would not only invite vandalism but result in a huge financial burden. All things considered, selling seemed the more desirable option, especially given the horror stories we had heard from friends who had rented their properties. When I asked the Lord if we should immediately list the house with a realtor, Allen received this verse from John 7:17(NIV): "If anyone chooses to do God's will, he will find out whether my teaching comes from God or whether I speak on my own." The Lord's point, spoken through the Apostle John, was that we were to set our hearts on doing God's will, acting in faith, and that, by doing so, we would be given understanding. Unfortunately, we always wanted things to be the other way around. Driven by our insecurity, we insisted on understanding *before* we acted!

7-10-92

In the meantime, we had the further challenge of needing to find a place to live in Ambridge. With the start of school only five weeks away, all of the other incoming students had already made living arrangements. Some, in fact, had been settled in for weeks, and there was precious little housing left. To make matters worse, in trying to rent, we also had the disadvantage of owning two cats. We began frequent contact with the seminary's Housing Coordinator, but nothing became available. The following verses came to mind: "Peter said to him, 'We have left everything to follow you!' 'I tell you the truth,' Jesus replied, 'no one who has left *home* or brothers or sisters or mother or father or children or fields for me and the gospel will fail to receive a hundred times as much in this present age (homes, brothers, sisters, mothers, children and fields--and with them persecutions) and in the age to come, eternal life.'" (Mark 10:28-30, NIV)

It was comforting to be reassured that our obedience would result in multiplied recompense, though I am also certain that a part of us did not really believe it would be so, and we surely didn't know when or how. But it was sobering and, indeed, troubling to be reminded that along with the blessings promised for following Jesus would come persecutions, something we had always assumed to be the consequence of laboring in dangerous and far-away mission fields.

Lastly, Allen described this vision: "I saw a book-shaped object which was acting like a lamp, shedding light beneath itself." This image clearly seemed to be a visual depiction of the words of Psalm 119:105(NIV): "Your word is a lamp to my feet and a light for my path." Whenever the path directly at our feet seemed dark, it was likely because we weren't allowing the light of God's word to shine upon it.

<u>7-12-92</u>

Allen wrote, "We are asking about the right price for our house when we put it on the market. Jan also asked again about the houses that I had looked at the other day in Ambridge. I thought I got the word *'dal,'* and I also received 1Thessalonians 3:4, which reads: "In fact, when we were with you, we kept telling you that we would be persecuted. And it turned out that way, as you well know."(NIV) St. Paul's words to the Thessalonians confirmed that we were indeed in for some difficulties! As usual, and perhaps fortunately, the Lord's full meaning was hidden from our view.

The word *"dal"* took a bit of research. I sensed that the word might be Hebrew, and, when I looked it up in the back of my concordance, I discovered, to my dismay, that it means "dangling, weak, lean, needy, or poor." The form of some of our intimated suffering began to take shape.

We resumed our prayer that night and Allen wrote, "We went out for dinner with Jan's father today, and we had an opportunity to talk about the strong possibility of our going to seminary. From his paternal posture, he naturally asked the question we've been asking: 'Where will it lead in terms of a job?' I had to say that I wasn't sure, though there were many possibilities. The truth is that I don't know at all, and I'm just trying to follow where it seems that God is leading. As we then started to pray, I was asking about our confusion of today, and for guidance. We asked about the sale of our house, and whether we were being foolish, and I heard, *'Many times my people have been foolish.'"* Even the most cursory reading of scripture will dramatically attest to the truth of that statement, so at least we were in good company!

7-13-92

After our morning's discussion, we arrived at the conclusion that we needed to act quickly on listing our house with a realtor. Later that evening, however, we had a funny and brisk exchange with the Lord. Allen wrote, "Jan is asking about the situation with the real estate people, and I heard, *'You are too anxious.'* Jan then asked for a word of wisdom about this whole process, and I heard, *'Don't worry.'* When Jan asked if there were some other means of acting that we weren't considering, I heard, *'It doesn't matter.'* Finally, as Jan then asked what all of this meant, I heard, *'Proceed as normal.'"*

This series of responses was both amusing and frustrating, for it seemed to contain two contradictory elements. First, the Lord seemed to be hinting that for the present, *nothing* we did with regard to the house would really make any difference. Secondly, despite this fact, we were apparently to proceed with whatever activities would be normal to anyone in our circumstances, including, for instance, listing the house!

I might add that while all of this mental and physical activity was going on surrounding our move, I was continuing with my process of inner healing. On this occasion, I was especially anxious about a session that was coming up shortly. Allen wrote, "As Jan asked about her inner healing session, I heard *'Do not fear, only believe.'* Later, I saw what looked like the mouth of a jar or bottle that had been turned upside down.'" I knew the image to be a directive from the Lord, albeit a painful one. I, as the bottle, was to completely pour out whatever thoughts, emotions, and confessions of my own sin were at issue during that session. Though this was never a pleasant exercise, I always found that the degree of healing I received was in direct proportion to my willingness to be obedient to this difficult task.

7-14-92

Allen wrote, "Jan and I are praying together, and we are asking the Lord how we can really know if we are doing is His will. I heard, *'Test it in the Book,'* and also, *'In many advisors there is wisdom.'"* Stated here again were the Lord's two fundamental methods for determining His will--both of which, unfortunately, we were still failing to utilize consistently. First, we were to diligently search His Word. Second, through prayer and discussion, we were to seek out the wisdom and counsel of other discerning members of the body of Christ. Immediately, the next scripture was given as confirmation: "From him the whole body, joined and held together by every supporting ligament, grows and builds itself up in love, as each part does its work." (Ephesians 4:16, NIV)

7-15-92

Allen wrote, "We decided last night, with much trepidation, to list our house. I don't know why there should be such fear associated with this process. It seems that we need to change, but our 'stuff' has such a hold on us. I feel a sense of adventure in the calling, but a tremendous fear of loss--of friends, of roots, and perhaps of identity."

Now, with so much needing to be done in order to leave, the pressures on us became intense. Indeed, time itself seemed to be accelerating. Though on one level we managed to maintain a certain degree of trust, there were many moments when we lapsed into fits of irritability and worry. Allen wrote, "Jan prayed that we have an incredible amount to do, and she asked for God's help." But to our surprise, help came in the form of these stern words of Paul to the Corinthians: "For I do not want you to be ignorant of the fact, brothers, that our forefathers were all under the cloud and that they all passed through the sea. They were all baptized into Moses in the cloud and in the sea. They all ate the same spiritual food and drank the same spiritual drink; for they drank from the spiritual rock that accompanied them, and that rock was Christ. Nevertheless, God was not pleased with most of them; their bodies were scattered over the desert. Now these things occurred as examples to keep us from setting our hearts on evil things as they did. (1 Corinthians 10:1-6, NIV)

The Lord wanted it made clear that even though we had been the recipients of incredible spiritual blessings, we would not be beyond the reach of His discipline if we incurred His displeasure through self-centered grumbling and wavering faith.

The Lord's very next word to us, however, revealed that He hadn't lost His sense of humor regarding our situation, for Allen heard Him exclaim, *"Geronimo!"* I was baffled, but Allen recalled that in World War II, paratroopers jumped from their planes with this shout. The Lord was clearly saying, "Just jump!" We laughed until our sides ached.

Later that evening, our prayer continued: "Jan began praying about our total dependence on God, and how we can so easily fall into depending on our possessions as our hedge against the world. We then asked God to help us let go of our material attachments to our property, even down to the shrubs and flowers we had planted. I heard, *'There is joy in heaven over the flowers.'*" It was beyond my comprehension to think that the planting of my little gardens over the years had produced joy in the heavenly realm!

7-16-92

We went to the home of friends for dinner, and afterwards settled into conversation and prayer about our plans. As I asked the Lord how we would know His will concerning renting or buying a house in Ambridge, Allen heard, *"It will be obvious. Follow.'"* Here was a good but deceptively simple piece of advice. So often we pressed for answers, when what we really needed to do was just continue on the path, watching, as we did so, which doors of opportunity opened, and which closed.

7-20-92

At this point, we had begun the exhausting process of cleaning the house and yard to make the property more presentable for showing. Yet at the same time, with only four weeks remaining until the start of school, we still had not acquired a place to live in Ambridge. The situation was nerve wracking, to say the least. At the end of our prayer time on this particular morning, Allen wrote: "I have a vivid sense of Christ's suffering and death on the cross for me, and I heard Him say, *'I risked.'"* Surely, if He could, so could we. Embarrassed, we asked ourselves why we were so continually obsessed with our own security.

7-21-92

In the process of sorting through possessions and cleaning out closets, I had amassed a sizable collection of miscellaneous objects that lay in a huge heap on the family room floor. What were we to do with it all? The obvious answer was to have a garage sale! For several days, I contemplated this daunting prospect but was too exhausted to organize it and acquire the necessary town permit, and it's the kind of thing I've never been the least bit good at, anyway. So, each day I would go downstairs and stare at the pile, the silent testimony to our acquisitive culture--but the pile only stared back. Finally, we prayed about it. Allen wrote, "Jan asked for help in getting rid of her stuff, and I heard a voice say softly, *'You can always give it away.'"* And so we did. We made an announcement and, in no time, friends and family appeared and carted off item after item until the pile dwindled to nothing. As each possession departed, we felt lighter and freer. In two days it was all gone, and we rejoiced at the wisdom of the Lord. Interestingly, I can't name a single item that was in that pile of stuff, and we never missed any of it for even a moment, so I guess we didn't need it!

<u>7-27-92</u>

The house had finally gone on the market, and there had been several showings, but nary a nibble of interest. Wrote Allen, "We are asking whether we should be waiting to sell the house, or whether we should just go, and trust that the house will be sold. Not by coincidence, we also asked again about the word *'dal.'* I got the phrase *'You're not reading the Book.'* Then, I saw what looked like a large spool with nothing on it.'"

The empty spool suggested that the Lord had perhaps come to the end of His patience--and, looking back, I don't blame Him! Again, it may have hinted that the spool of our own resources would run out. But if we had truly been "reading the Book," we would have been amply reminded that God frequently tested His people and taught them to trust by removing all other means of reliance. We would indeed be "dangling, thin, poor, lean, and needy." Though we didn't recognize it then, the Lord was fully intending that the spool of our time run out before any of the issues concerning our house were resolved.

At the end of our prayer time, the Lord shared two delightful visions: Allen wrote, "I seemed to see several women's faces, almost like statues, but with their hair blowing. Then, I saw a face that looked almost like a baby Statue of Liberty, but again with her hair blowing." These were stirring images, for I knew that they expressed the Lord's desire for me to be emotionally and spiritually *free.* When I later looked up the word "freedom" in my concordance, I was led to the following verse: "Now the Lord is the Spirit, and *where the Spirit of the Lord is, there is freedom.*" (2 Corinthians 3:17, NIV, italics mine) This verse makes the images all the more interesting, since the Greek word for spirit, *"pneuma,"* also means "breath" or "wind." The second image repeated the theme of the first, but with a specific emphasis. Here, the Lord seemed to be showing me that He meant for me to continue the process of allowing Him to free my inner child from the fears and bondage of my past. Scripture again came to mind: "For you did not receive a spirit that makes you a slave again to fear, but you received the Spirit of sonship. And by him we cry, '*Abba*, Father.'" (Romans 8:15, NIV)

As time went on, I slowly became aware that there was far more to this second image than I had initially imagined. Throughout my childhood, an unfortunate combination of emotional abuse and lopsided doctrine had served to distort my understanding of God as my Heavenly Father. Now, as the months unfolded, and the Spirit's inner healing work continued, I began to see that my badly skewed view of God had only added to my emotional pain by keeping me from the relationship I needed most. It was to this intimacy I was now being called.

In the midst of this new call, I also had the challenging task of informing my parents of our decision and of our imminent departure. But what once would have been a formidable assignment had now been made oddly easier by the experiences of the previous months, for I had been forcibly disavowed of my emotional need for their approval, at least in this situation. I had learned a hard lesson the hard way.

My father accepted the news of our leaving with his typical mixture of benign acquiescence and resignation. While on the one hand he understood and seemed proud of the new possibilities in store for us, he was, I'm sure, saddened at the thought of the physical separation. And, too, he was no doubt inwardly aware that the ensuing changes would carry us down a path from which we would never return--at least in the same way, or as the same people. I also went to the nursing home and explained our situation briefly to my mother. Given her failing hearing and speech, it was becoming more difficult to communicate with her. Nonetheless, she seemed to comprehend what I had said, receiving the news with little comment, although I think that she too was proud of us. The reactions of my parents to our news offered me a valuable reminder: despite the years of pain and dysfunction in our relationship, the jagged peaks of anger and the plunging valleys of despair, when all was said and done, there did remain the underlying bedrock of love. But I also noted with thanksgiving that, while I appreciated their tacitly expressed support, I was no longer dependent on it.

7-30-92

As yet we had no offers on our house, and we were becoming irritable and discouraged, but a conversation with a friend revealed that she and her husband had some serious interest in renting it and were coming to look it over. We began to fasten our hopes on this possibility, especially since this couple would have been ideal renters, but the prospect still left us with some difficult financial issues. That evening, we brought the matter before the Lord.

Allen wrote, "As I prayed about my concern over money, and what we should do with the house, and how we were going to finance everything, I heard the word *'Wait,'* followed by the words 'Jehovah *Jireh*' *(meaning God sees and provides)* and *'Water from the rock.'*" Waiting, of course, was the last thing we wanted to do. But the Lord had much to teach us that only our waiting would accomplish, for trust was ever the heart of the matter. Would we put our confidence in Jehovah Jireh, that same Lord who *saw* Abraham's need and *provided*--at the last moment-- the sacrificial ram, in Isaac's stead? And was He not the one who poured forth water from the rock in the wilderness for the parched Israelites, when Moses spoke to it? Not by accident, as I next prayed about how I continually fell back into grumbling and insecurity, Allen heard, *'You're coming out of Egypt.'* The Lord's comment further identified us with the insecure and impatient Israelites, but it also revealed His gracious understanding of our struggle to break free from the bondage of our past. Though He periodically expressed impatience with us, He generally displayed a remarkable tolerance towards our foibles and frailties. He knew we were in the midst of a wilderness experience, since it was He who had led us there. When I refer to God's impatience, I don't mean so in our human and fallen sense. God's "impatience" is rather a function of His longing for our betterment.

Finally, the entire message came full circle with this verse from Romans 10:11(NIV): "As the scripture says, 'Anyone who trusts in him will never be put to shame.'" The issue of trust was to loom larger still as the date of our departure drew closer.

7-31-92

There were now only two-and-a-half weeks remaining until school started, and things were anything but rosy. Our potential renters were still undecided, there were no buyers in sight, the house was far from packed, and we still had no place to live in Ambridge. And, of course, our business situation seemed terrible. In our worst moments, we resorted to verbally bashing each other, and Allen wrote:

> "I know that there must have been times in my life when I've felt worse than I do at the moment, but I can't remember them. I am worried about the finances of this whole situation, and I have no answers. All of my resources are expended and my confidence is running on empty. I know we are called to trust in God and not in ourselves or the world, but I just don't see how all of this can happen. Jan is upset, and I'm upset, and nothing is going well. I started to pray, asking the Lord how we can possibly do this move, and I saw an odd sort of line drawing that I couldn't make out. However, some of the items were being filled in and were almost discernible. Then, I saw two slightly converging lines, with the space between them narrowing."

These two images were clear enough for, in different ways, they said the same thing: the picture was being filled in, and things were beginning to come together. Though we had trouble seeing this with our natural eyes, we now knew we were to accept it as a spiritual reality.

Finally, I turned to the problem of my still-surfacing anger. Allen wrote, "Jan asked about her temper, and how she tries to control it, but can't. I heard, *'You can't do it in your own strength,'* followed by *'When you're worrying, you're not doing what I need done.'"* A succinct scriptural summation of these two statements was then given in the following verse: "I can do everything through him who gives me strength." (Philippians 4:13, NIV) Over the next two weeks, it would become abundantly clear that it was the Lord's strength, and not our own, that was sustaining us.

<u>8-2-92</u>

Allen wrote, "We asked if this process that we are in is truly the Lord's will for our lives—and, if not, what His will *is*. He replied, *'Don't resist.'* Jan then asked how she was going to have the stamina to do all that needed to be done, and I heard, *'That's part of what this is all about.'"* The Lord's beginning admonition was firm and straightforward, but I found His second remark to be rather mysterious, and I pondered it for some time. I understood that the Lord was reiterating our need to draw on *His* strength, but He also seemed to be saying that I would actually be physically, emotionally, and spiritually energized by the process of packing and leaving. This I would have to see to believe!

Meanwhile, no housing had as yet surfaced in Ambridge. Initially, we had planned on driving back out there in order to pursue the search in person, but we now realized that with the start of school just days away, we had neither the time nor the energy to make two exhausting trips within such a short period of time. And we still had the entire house to pack up! The matter was weighing heavily on our minds, and Allen wrote, "Jan asked about going to Ambridge in the next few days, and whether we are to buy or rent. I thought I heard, *'You can't buy,'* followed by the word *'Joy.'* Then, I seemed to hear *'You will be blessed.'"*

We welcomed the Lord's first words with some relief. At last we had definite instructions, and could act accordingly, though it would take us nearly a year to fully understand just what He had meant by *"being blessed."* When we did, we would see that what had appeared to be a brusque and matter-of-fact reply regarding our housing was in fact the wrapping concealing what would later be a wonderful gift:

a house of our own provided in an utterly unexpected and seemingly impossible way.

The second word, *"joy,"* was a deceptively simple one, for behind it laid a profound theology. On several recent occasions, the Lord had spoken this word to us, and it would become a major theme for our journey, but I was still so emotionally wounded that I was unable to grasp just what He was saying. The same was true for the promise of blessing, but, as time went on, this message of joy and blessing would reveal itself to be a remarkable understatement.

<u>8-3-92</u>

Allen wrote, "It doesn't seem real that in two weeks, if all goes as planned, we will be moved and in Ambridge, just starting orientation. I am under such pressure that I can't imagine how some people do this process every few years. We prayed about how we were going to accomplish this move, since it seems so difficult at this point: house not sold, and no place to live in Ambridge yet." However, the Lord didn't seem the least bit concerned with those nagging details. Instead, Allen was given Malachi 4:2(NIV): "But for you who revere my name, the sun of righteousness will rise with healing in its wings. And you will go out and leap like calves released from the stall." While this prophecy will not find its complete fulfillment until the age to come, the verse spoke to us again of the healing, the freedom, and the exuberant, kick-up-your-heels *joy* that the Lord had planned for us. The point of it all was that, like penned up young calves, we were being released from the restraints of our old lives to frolic in a new pasture.

Later that night Allen continued, "This has been a day of frustration and blessing. I have done a lot of packing, despite the fact that I didn't know where we were going to live in Ambridge. But at 6 o'clock tonight, something perfect finally came together: a nice house, just two blocks from Trinity, became available for us to rent. Now all we have is a hundred other little things to resolve, but I believe that the Lord's hand is on this, and as we are faithful and obedient, we can trust in Him for provision."

The house was one that had previously been unavailable to us because of our cats, charming creatures though they were. But, unbeknown to us, the owners had graciously relented, and consequently, just ten days before the start of classes, we suddenly had a delightful little house just a stone's throw from school! We made note of three spiritual lessons that the Lord no doubt desired to teach us through this experience. First, He often waits until the very last minute to come through, in order to teach us patience and trust. Second, contrary to appearances, He is in absolute control of our circumstances. And third, His desire is to bless us in ways that we never could have imagined, and which far exceed anything we might have arranged through our own efforts.

Our prayer time closed with the following. Allen wrote, "I heard the words *'I want you to preach,'* and then I saw a large, vertically striped balloon, rising above some puffy white clouds.'" Allen often made small sketches of the images he saw and when I looked at this cheery little drawing, I instantly found myself humming the words, "Up, up, and away in my beautiful balloon!" We were indeed on the verge of a great adventure.

<u>8-4-92</u>

The next few days were consumed with packing, and it was an interesting exercise, to say the least! Allen wrote, "It's been a hectic day of trying to tie up many loose ends, as well as of packing some of the more difficult items. I still have the garage to tackle, and I'm dreading that, since it's such a mess. This experience is a kind of catharsis, as I am going through all of the accumulation of the past fifteen years, throwing away lots of stuff, and dealing with lots of emotions. I have clearly seen my financial foolishness as I've done this cleaning, but thank God that He is a God of grace and mercy."

What's more, despite the sizable and growing stack of packed boxes that now sat in our basement, we were still plagued with recurring questions as to whether we were doing the right thing. The Lord addressed our doubts, confirmed our decision, and even reminded us of His sense of humor with this verse from Ezekiel 12:7(NIV): "So I did as

I was commanded. During the day I brought out my things packed for exile. Then in the evening I dug through the wall with my hands. I took my belongings out at dusk, carrying them on my shoulders while they watched." We burst into laughter, for apart from "digging through the wall with our hands," Ezekiel's words were aptly descriptive of our own activities. Indeed, like him, our actions would prove to have prophetic significance, for our leaving was to be a sign of faith and obedience to all those who knew us.

God's closing words to us were these: *"Hold fast. Thy help is in the name of the Lord."*

<u>8-5-92</u>

We now had barely over a week remaining until our departure. To the packing had been added all of the seemingly endless organizational details concerned with moving. Should we hire a moving van, or attempt the move ourselves? For economy's sake, Allen opted for a rental truck, and busied himself with making those arrangements. His father and his brother Bruce were recruited to drive the truck, while we would ride in our car. Next, utilities needed to be cancelled, services notified, and mail rerouted, and so on went the list. As one might expect, there were moments when we were overcome with exhaustion, but on this particular evening, Allen heard the Lord offer, *"This weariness is not unto death, but life."*

<u>8-6-92</u>

After the first brief flurry of browsers, all activity regarding our house sale had dwindled to nothing, and neither had our potential renters made a firm commitment. Consequently, all we could do was to repeatedly submit the matter to prayer. Allen wrote, "We gave thanks to God for His blessings, and then Jan asked what we were to do with the house. As she did do, I received this scripture: "It does not, therefore, depend on man's desire or effort, but on God's mercy." (Romans 9:16, NIV) How often we needed to be reminded that, try as we might, we were not in charge!

<u>8-9-92</u>

This would be our last Sunday at our church, and they blessed us with a surprise going away party. We had a sense of excitement and anticipation, but we were sad at leaving so many friends who had been close to us. We would return to visit, but their lives and ours would now, and likely forever, proceed apart from one another. A card from one dear friend, echoing the title of a popular movie, had affectionately dubbed our departure "Al and Jan's most excellent adventure." Of course, we were far from the first to engage such a call, such a major life commitment, and, in truth, compared to the lives of countless saints, this was pretty mild stuff. Nonetheless, many people commented that they could never have done what we were doing.

<u>8-11-92</u>

Allen recorded these words on the evening before our last day at home:

> "I don't think I can ever recall going through such a range of emotions as I've experienced over the last few days. There are so many people whom it is difficult to leave. There is a sense of excitement about going, but also a sense of uncertainty about the future. I feel that it's all in the Lord's hands, but it's so hard to let go of what we know and grasp something unfamiliar. I had always thought of myself as being adventurous, but it is clear that I'm not. I'm number than I am anything else right now. I've done so much packing and trying to sort things out that my mind is in a fog. This whole process of cleaning out my past is very painful, but also freeing. It is rare, I think, that we have opportunities to assess our lives in the kind of depth occasioned by this major move and life change. It is frightening to see how much of my ability I've wasted on things that ultimately count

for little. I guess that is what we are really doing here--
trying to make our lives make sense by being obedient
to God."

Meanwhile, after much deliberation, our potential renters had finally decided that they were desirous of a longer-term lease, and so we were left with the prospect of leaving the house empty. Looking back, we were eventually to realize that this had likely been the Lord's intention from the beginning, but we had no such benefit of hindsight at the time. Hence, we were prompted to seek the Lord once more. Allen wrote, "We prayed about the house, and about our whole financial picture, and I saw a representation of a rider on a horse. They appeared to be jumping over something." This image seemed to convey the Lord's reassurance that we, as the rider, would manage this hurdle. But as happened so many times, it was one thing to receive this message with our intellects, and quite another to truly believe it at the emotional level. Allen then continued, "We prayed for a safe trip for all of us, especially for my father and Bruce, who have a two-way trip. Jan then prayed for healing in her abdomen (I remembered my last ride to Ambridge!), and I heard the words *'An image.'* Then I heard, *'There is power and healing in this process.'"* The Lord's first words continued to remain largely a mystery to me, but the significance of His second statement would soon begin to become evident.

<u>8-12-92</u>

I had been blessed by the assistance of two dear friends who, knowing my post-surgical state, had arrived earlier in the week to pack dishes, glassware, pots, and pans while I watched apologetically from a chair, but now the day had come for the house to be emptied of its contents. The large yellow Ryder truck stood in the driveway with its ramp-mouth down, waiting to swallow our worldly goods. As the day wore on, an energetic crew was assembled, and by mid-afternoon, some were busily packing up anything that had not yet found its way into a box, while others were tackling the furniture and appliances. Now, too, all of those basement cartons had to be loaded. There were seventy boxes in all.

True to Ezekiel's prophecy, the work was finished just as it was getting dark! Pizza had been ordered for the famished and sweaty crew, and we all stood in the driveway devouring it, while Allen and I marveled at the fact that everything we owned was now in that funny yellow truck.

By the time everyone had said their good-byes and headed home, and we had attended to last minute details, it was nearly midnight. We had left one bare mattress on the floor in one of the bedrooms, and it was onto this that we finally collapsed. As I lay there in the dark, more tired than I had ever been in my entire life, it seemed, I sighed heavily and wondered out loud one last time, "O Lord, have we done the right thing?" In a flash, Allen heard a voice in a heavily Jewish accent reply, *"Oy! How could it be wrong?"* The Lord's zany humor was, as usual, exactly what we needed, and we laughed ourselves to sleep.

<u>8-13-92</u>

Given the length of our ride, our plans were to be on the road by 7 A.M. On awakening, we had a second chance to laugh at ourselves, for in our packing zeal, Allen had left himself literally nothing to wear! Hence, his first order of business was to borrow some clothes from his father.

I quickly dressed, rounded up the two cats, and put them in their carriers. They were not amused. Then, in the gray dawn light, I walked through the house and said my farewell to each room, thanking the Lord for its memories, and for the gift of the house itself--our home for the last fifteen years.

Suddenly, we were on our way. The car pulled out of the driveway behind the Ryder truck, as I took one last glance back at the house. Allen drove, and I sat in the front seat, while Melissa and Spuds occupied the back. I checked my watch: it was exactly 7 A.M.

For the first two hours of the trip, the cats loudly wailed their disapproval of the whole affair, but eventually they resigned themselves to their fate, and thereafter merely chose to glower at me when I peered into their carriers. My chief memory of the day's drive consists of rolling down the road on a sweltering August day behind that big yellow truck that contained everything we owned. As I pondered unpacking it all again, I wondered what our rented house would look like. I felt ever so much like Abraham, to whom the Lord had said, "Leave your country, your people, and your father's household and go to the land I will show you." (Genesis 12:1, NIV)

8

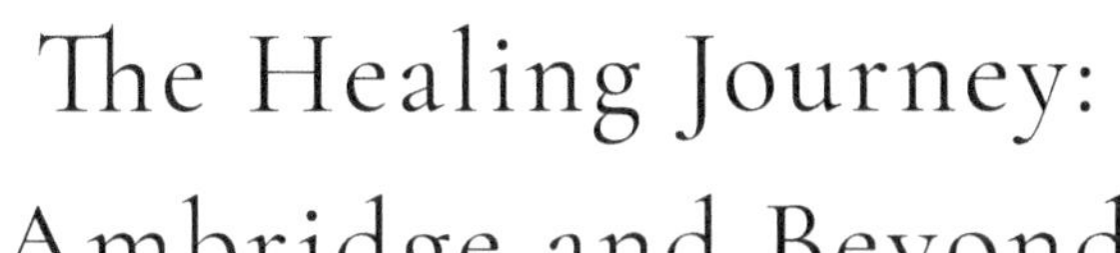

The Healing Journey: Ambridge and Beyond

It was 8:30 that Thursday evening and just getting dark when we finally pulled up across from our three-story brick row house on Church Street. There we were--four road-weary travelers and two sullen felines. After fourteen hours on a steamy highway, we were all exhausted, and Allen and I commented that our earlier sense of adventure had, at that moment, all but evaporated. All we wanted now boiled down to a bed and a shower, but we first had that large yellow truck to unload.

Feeling an odd mixture of anticipation and displacement, I opened the car door and stepped out into the still stifling heat, stretching my aching legs, neck, and back. Then, turning, I stood transfixed for a moment, gazing up at the strangely high and narrow brick row house that we had rented, sight unseen, which was to be our home for the coming year. As my eyes centered on the door of our little house, I noted that we were about to cross both a literal and a symbolic threshold. Our "most excellent adventure" was now more than an idea, a possibility, or a hope. Ready or not, it was all about to begin in earnest. Though our spiritual journey, begun some years before, had already brought us a long way, in many ways it, too, was just beginning.

My fond musings came to a quick halt, however, with Allen's sharp reminder that we needed to start unpacking the truck. Our first task was to get the house keys from Richard and Barbara, our new neighbors in the row house next door. To our dismay, we quickly realized that we had failed to have the gas, electricity, and water turned back on. Worse yet, that couldn't be done until Monday, the same morning on which registration and orientation were starting. Richard and Barbara gave us flashlights and candles, and it was by the light of those that we first saw the inside of our house. Shortly, a team of four or five fellow seminarians, aptly dubbed "Bridgers," arrived to help us move in. We all worked feverishly to empty the truck, as Al's dad and brother would need to head back early the next morning to return it to the rental office. (I would add here that Allen's brother later offered to rent our now empty house.) Though it could have been seen as a minor disaster, we were somehow able to see the humor and the adventure in it all, and that whole crazy night has given us many laughs over the years. For the next several days, we ate at restaurants, showered at a neighbor's house, and functioned solely with flashlights and candles at home.

Just hours earlier, we had left behind all that was familiar. If I hadn't been so exhausted and anxious to unpack, I might have paused to give a moment's reflection on the sharp contrast in environment with the home from which we had departed that morning, for the two settings could hardly have been more different. Southwick, Massachusetts, a small New England town on the edge of the Berkshires, is a picture postcard of rolling hills, winding country roads, lakes, dairy farms, and tobacco fields. Yet, I had often and, increasingly, of late, felt lonely, isolated, out of place, and at loose ends. Here in Ambridge, however, I was met with narrow streets, some still cobbled, of tightly compacted houses constructed in the early 1900's by the steel mill owners for their workers. Whereas our house in Southwick had a large wooded lot, our Ambridge rental was but an arm's length from the houses on either side. What's more, we were in easy walking distance of the seminary and the library, the post office, the grocery store, the pharmacy, the dentist, and much more. Some of our new neighbors were long-standing residents, while others were fellow seminarians and their families, and walking down the sidewalk or even simply stepping outside nearly always resulted in a greeting or a conversation. Most significant, however, would be the physical and spiritual closeness of the seminary community and its vibrant life, in which we would quickly find ourselves immersed. These differences would prove to be striking metaphors for the profound and happy changes our lives were about to undergo, for God knows what He is about. In a few days, we would be sitting in our classes, which would ultimately include theology, Old and New Testament history, church history, apologetics, and Biblical Greek and Hebrew. Besides these would be weekday morning chapel, interactions with several new churches, and youth and pastoral ministry training. And then there was life in the heart of an old steel mill town, introduction to the rich history and culture of Pittsburgh, and daily blessing in the fellowship of the seminary community, many of whom lived within walking distance of us. It was exactly what we needed.

However, the next year was to prove both a marvelous blessing and a great challenge, as I now dug with diligence into the process of pursuing *emotional* healing. Allen, of course, would have his own work to do in that regard. We would also find ourselves enormously stretched by a return to an academic environment, and an intense one at that. Indeed, a senior classmate and former physician commented that seminary was far tougher than medical school had been!

Ultimately, we would be in Ambridge for four years, as we pursued Allen's fuller call to ordination and full-time ministry. However, we have chosen to limit our narrative portion by briefly scanning across the map of that first semester's journey, both of healing and of exploration of mission, ministry, and purpose. This portion of our journey is, of course, uniquely ours, but, while our stories are hopefully interesting, they are only edifying if there is a wider spiritual application--an insight into the way God works, and how He desires our lives to work.

The months that followed our coming to Ambridge were naturally filled with the emotional ups and downs of having left all that was familiar to us. Not long after our arrival, our pastor, who was in town for a meeting, stopped by to visit and attend chapel with us. I experienced a roller-coaster of emotions: joy when he came and home-sickness when he left, for he symbolized everyone and everything that had been our life. What's more, I continued to struggle greatly with the inner healing process, often feeling that my progress looked more like a pathetic zigzag than a straight road forward. Anxiety also mounted as I feared interacting with my mother on our first trip home for a visit, but the Lord reassured me, saying, *"Remember that your mother doesn't have the last word, but I do."*

Allen, of necessity, was most intensely focused on his schoolwork and on other practical matters related to house and finances, but, on August 18th, as we asked the Lord for help with all of these issues, Allen instead heard Him say, *"You're too insistent."* And so we were. As Allen wrote, "It is so hard not to live in what the world calls reality, but instead to trust in God's spiritual reality. Why am I so chained to the world by what I think I need?" In an effort to assuage our anxiety regarding our various situations, we were constantly trying to press for *answers,* when the Lord simply wanted *faith and obedience.* In hindsight, it is evident that our whole experience, specifics aside, was largely designed as an adventure in trust. Abraham would have understood.

On August 20th, as Allen was pondering his need to choose his courses the next day, he had a vision of a *pail.* At chapel the next morn-ing, the homilist related the story of two men who were in a small boat off the coast of South America. They were dying of thirst when a large boat came by, and the sailors called to the men to put their *bucket* into the water and drink. As it happened, they were in the fresh water that flowed from the Amazon River twenty miles out into the sea! This, we felt, was encouragement from the Lord that, in terms of both academics and preparation for ministry, we were in the right place and doing the right thing.

On the 24th, however, Allen was still agonizing over academics, as well as over our ongoing financial commitments, as we had some savings, but no consistent income. He was still looking for *answers,* but, this time, the Lord's simple counter was this *question: "Can you imagine how much I love you?"* (The short answer, of course, was, and is, "Probably not!")

This was followed by Colossians 1, verses 9 and 10. Here, Paul, (along with Timothy), writes this message of encouragement to that church: "For this reason, since the day we heard about you, we have not stopped praying for you and asking God to fill you with the knowledge of his will through all spiritual wisdom and understanding. And we pray this in order that you may live a life worthy of the Lord and may please him in every way: bearing fruit in every good work, growing in the knowledge of God..." (NIV)

First, we needed to be *assured,* not only that God loved us, but that *others* loved us and were *praying* for us, as well. Though I missed the fuller meaning then, it strikes me now that those prayers didn't stop but continue to this day in the communion of saints, including perhaps, even Paul and Timothy themselves! As Shakespeare wrote, "There are more things in heaven and earth, Horatio, than are dreamt of in your philosophy."

Second, despite the Lord's ongoing assurances, we needed constant reminders that our situation wasn't about our current struggles with coursework and money, but about the larger reasons behind why we were there. Just *how* were we to live a life worthy of the Lord, pleasing Him, bearing fruit, and growing in knowledge of Him? The image that followed gave us some clues. It consisted of two large stone idols next to one another, with two people who had been tied to them being released. After that, Allen saw an image of a man in a spacesuit, and he commented that the man looked like himself! Clearly, the message was of *deliverance* from spiritual, emotional, and financial bondage, followed by the challenge and exhilaration of *exploration.*

However, as is so often true of the Lord, His gentle exhortations are often coupled with warnings. Hence, the scripture that followed was Isaiah 28, verse 12: "to whom he said, 'This is the resting place, let the weary rest;'" and "'This is the place of repose'"—"but they would not listen." (NIV)

So much had happened in our first two weeks in Ambridge that we now found ourselves in a rather odd space. We already felt quite disconnected from our old lives, and yet there was a strange unreality to this new life. Our prayer was that it would all make sense--that we would come to see how we were serving God in that place, and how we would do so beyond it. In the meantime, all we did know was that this was to be a time away, a place to heal, and a preparation for our future. It was a gift and a grace, and it was necessary, not only for our growth, but, for our survival, in the fullest sense of that word. The Lord's further advice was eminently practical: *"Take advantage of the opportunities, and don't worry!"*

In that light, as Allen began to participate in worship services that were offered as part of his training, he found some things to be un-helpful and uninspiring. When we prayed about this, the Lord offered, *"There is blessing in all things."* The word was a good reminder that what we see as obstacles might be seen as opportunities. He also gave Allen Hebrews 11:1: "Now faith is being sure of what we hope for and certain of what we do not see." (NIV) What follows is a chapter-long record of those Old Covenant heroes whose faith fueled the Biblical narrative of salvation, typically with heroic courage, and sometimes through horrific suffering--things that made our challenges seem tiny and insignificant in comparison.

At the same time, while Allen remained preoccupied with school-work and field parish work, and while both of us continued to agonize over finances, I was still wrestling with my family situation at home, and with inner healing issues. The following dream, recorded on Sep-tember 5th, vividly underscores the kind of damage suffered and my feelings of helplessness and anger:

> "In the dream, Allen and I had recently gone a distance
> away to live, but had come back for a visit. We were at
> the house where I had lived as a teenager, and we were
> in the kitchen. My mother was also there, and it seems
> as though she was ironing. I was hungry, and decided
> to make a meal. Searching through cupboards, I found

the ingredients to make spaghetti tossed with a spinach sauce. As I began to cook, I sensed growing irritation and disapproval from my mother. At last, I combined the ingredients in a large bowl to be served, but at that point my mother came over and got directly involved. She took a small portion of food out of the large bowl, placed it in a smaller serving bowl, and placed a large pat of butter in it, which I did not wish to eat. Then she told us that the smaller dish was all we could have. At the same time, she demanded that I determine the amounts of the various ingredients I had used, pro-rate them, and pay her. I felt a familiar sense of hurt, puzzlement, rage, frustration, and despair. Allen and I had planned after the meal to go out to visit a friend. I don't remember that we ate the food at all, but now I felt guilty about dirtying the kitchen, and decided to simply wash the dishes and leave, not even going to visit the friend, but returning directly home. My father was vaguely present during this latter portion of the dream, but said nothing, seeming to tacitly support my mother. I felt humiliation and defeat, but made no effort to ex-press my feelings. I did the dishes in a spirit of despair, resignation, and suppressed rage."

I wrote in response, "Lord, it is evident from this dream that there are still issues of anger and hurt to be resolved and healed. I ask you to come into these areas, take the pain and anger, and help me to forgive." Indeed, for those of us still wounded, we must deliberately align our wills to God's, lest our anger, bitterness, and lack of forgiveness block our own healing. Here again, focus on *others* has to be at the heart of both their healing and our own.

Sometime later, I had another striking dream related to my inner healing struggles: "I dreamed that I was sleeping in my bed in the house in Ambridge. In the dream, I heard what sounded like someone washing a window, and I "awoke" to see where the sound was coming from. As I did so, I saw my mother standing in the upstairs hall, with her back turned, washing the hall window. I saw her face in profile, and she seemed to be much younger, perhaps about 40. The following night I prayed, asking the Lord about this and other dreams I had had in which my mother seemed to be in her forties. The Lord replied, *"It's your mother in you."* This dream aptly conveyed the level of dysfunction and pain in our relationship. From an emotional and psychological standpoint, I found it fascinating, not to mention both helpful and disturbing, to contemplate the idea that my issues were the result of having "internalized" my mother, but that is just part of the human condition. I hesitate to write about and revisit these issues, but I know that there is healing in writing, as well as the hope that others may benefit.

Meanwhile, September 7th brought two words. First came this: *"Seek knowledge rightly, and I will bless."* The message was clear and sobering. In the seminary environment, it was easy to get caught up in the pressure of academics for its own sake, but academics without purpose, without *missionary* zeal, was not only pointless, but was displeasing to God. The second and related word was this: *"There is no joy over those who perish."* Those eight words were a reminder and an encapsulation of our mission, and of the purpose behind it all: the eternal destiny of mankind, for which Christ had come, suffered, and died.

Allen kept a daily journal of his thoughts and our lives during this time, and I am astounded by the fullness and busyness of every aspect of it, whether social, academic, ecclesiastic, or ministerial. What's more, a significant part of these experiences, especially for Allen, necessarily involved constantly processing and assessing everything in terms of our vocations and our future lives. What would be helpful for us and for others and what would not be?

And, of course, we lived amongst a community of seminary families who were all doing the same things, so there was a rich sense of communion, commonality, and support. Allen noted that he felt he was being put in places where he could not only minister, but also *receive* ministry. We were all happy, excited, invigorated, stretched, positive, and challenged--and most of us were more or less broke. But we were on mission, and we knew why, though we didn't know the specifics of our calls. Consequently, we were also nervous, confused, and uncertain about our futures, though we somehow knew that the Lord's hand was on it all. Our lives were up in the air, in the same way that a Ferris wheel, or roller coaster ride take you up in the air. The view is great, you know you're going to come back down safely, and it's all fun, in a scary sort of way--but your stomach is going to drop on the way down, and you might hear yourself screaming. As I have often told my religious education students concerning life, "If it's not scary, it's not an adventure."

Nonetheless, the inner struggle was still very real, and Allen often lamented that he felt so controlled by the material world around him that he feared it was interfering with his ability to hear God's guidance. At the same time, he also wrote that it was all too easy to get caught up in the patterns of student life and lose perspective on the whole experience.

Other issues in our own lives were also at work, and September 14th found Allen writing the following: "Sometimes I feel like I'm just starting to understand my life at a time when most people are planning for retirement. I know that God has a plan for both Jan and I and that we must be obedient to fulfill that plan. I am constantly worried about money, and though I know I must trust in the Lord, the bills keep coming in and I don't have what I need to pay them. I guess I really must live what God keeps calling us to--a life of trust and faith. I know it's the only way to live, but it's certainly extraordinarily hard to give up the desire to control--the feeling that if I don't do it, who will? I praise God that He is sovereign."

The next day, the Lord gave us two scriptures concerning how we were to regard *home*. In Jeremiah 29:4-7, the prophet exhorts the Jewish exiles in Babylon to settle where they now found themselves, meaning that they were to build houses, plant gardens and eat their produce, marry and have children, and even pray for the prosperity of that city.

In other words, they were to make Babylon their new home, in the earthly sense, and they were to be at peace with that and succeed where they were. After all, anything less would leave them frustrated, restless, unproductive, and unhappy. But Ephesians 2:6 was also given, and there, Paul reminds the church that, spiritually, they were *already* seated with Christ in the heavenly realms. The application, it seems, was this: we were now to accept Ambridge as our physical home, prosper there, and pray for all there, while also recognizing that our spiritual home was heaven. It's a good recipe for finding happiness, wherever we are.

Not by coincidence, on September 18th, we drove "home" for my doctor's appointment and a visit with family. Allen wrote: "Here we are in Southwick, Lord, dealing with many issues in our lives. It is so difficult to trust. We feel both lost without our material anchors and constrained by them. The only anchor that we can trust, Lord, is You, and we know that, yet there is a sense in which our identity comes from what we have, and we seem to grab onto things to affirm our position. I feel an awful sense of frustration as I try to find meaning in what I do, for the only meaning comes as a part of Your plan. Help me to focus solely on You for my meaning, Lord. I need Your guidance and Your loving grace."

Following this, Allen wrote that he thought he saw two shapes, like truncated pyramids, with one smaller than the other. They were side by side on a plain, flat white surface, and there was a light coming from above them and casting shadows. The two pyramids, it seems, represented Allen and I, and were a reminder that, emotionally and spiritually, we were still in bondage, still "in Egypt." That image was followed by one of a woman in a white dress with a strong blue pattern, standing with arms outstretched. At the time, the identity of the woman eluded us, but it now seems clear, from her emblematic colors and her loving invitation, that she was the Blessed Virgin Mary, our gracious spiritual mother. John 4:21, Jesus' words to the Samaritan woman, followed: "Jesus declared, 'Believe me, woman, a time is coming when you will worship the Father neither on this mountain nor in Jerusalem.'" (NIV) This image and this verse were only two of the many allusions to Mary, and to the Catholic Church, that we received during these early years, and which we would only later recognize, as we read back through our journals from the time preceding our conversion! The Master Gardener had been sowing these seeds all along, but, by His design, we had not yet been able to discern the nature of the plants, nor their fruit.

Meanwhile, as I was processing my own emotional responses to being "home," as well as the nature of my personal calling, Allen thought he got Psalm 78, verses 2-4. It read, "I will open my mouth in parables, I will utter hidden things, things from of old--what we have heard and known, what our fathers have told us. We will not hide them from their children; we will tell the next generation the praiseworthy deeds of the Lord, his power and the wonders he has done." (NIV) The Bible study question for those verses asks, "Who is the keeper of your family stories and traditions?" Many years later, I sit in amazement as I read those words from the vantage of my clear call to write, and of our resulting books and their many stories!

On our return from our visit back "home," I wrote this reflection in my own journal: "The visit was fraught with intense emotions having to do with home, house, parents, friends, church, and doctor. It was extremely strange to be home, and yet not have it be home, to drive by our house and know that someone else was living in it, to be visitors at our own church. I felt displaced and detached from many things that, only a few weeks ago, were my total life. I am increasingly aware that it is unlikely that we will ever return there to live."

This time in seminary would continue to be a time of fear and a sense of high adventure, of hope and confusion, of joy and exhaustion, of choices to be made and demands to be met.

On September 27th, Allen wrote: "In some ways I can't even comprehend the change that's come over my life. I blink, and here I am in Ambridge. I've always had trouble adapting to new things, Lord, as You know. I try to defend myself by putting up walls, even if I initiated the new thing. I always think it will be easy to change, but it never is. Lord, help me to serve You properly." The Lord's immediate response was, *"Feed My lambs."* It was an assignment, a commission. Shortly after, however, and true to his above lament, Allen instead found himself praying for guidance about the sale of our house. To our chagrin, the Lord quickly countered with this conditional, fill-in-the-blanks admonition: *"Unless you want Me more than______________"*

Meanwhile, the next little exchange shows just how well I was doing with *my* part regarding the above advice: When I prayed for help with writing an Old Testament paper, along with my frustration over being stressed academically, and not really doing ministry, the Lord said, *"You are in the right place."* I then asked if I had been called there primarily to do academic work, and He said, *"I called you here for training."* Last, when I again complained about the pressure of doing the schoolwork, He offered, *"Don't compare yourself."* Apparently He knew I had been, and He also knew that that was a large part of my problem, though it was a new and startling insight for me.

Not long afterwards, however, I again queried the Lord regarding my purpose in Ambridge, and this time, He focused on another, but also much-needed dimension of my task: *"You are seeking joy."* Here, I was reminded that my, and our purposes, would continue to be strongly connected with our work of inner healing. Now, too, the Lord returned to the subject of our ministry, with the words, *"Be about My work."* When I next asked if my courses would be useful in that endeavor, Allen saw a row of shapes like English muffins which seemed to be splitting (!), and he got a sense that those referred to rightly dividing the word of truth (See 2 Timothy, 2:15) The Lord explained, *"If you're going to war, you need the armor."* He was returning, yet again, to the intimate connections between hearing Him, healing, discerning truth, and purpose.

However, the following day found us praying about our financial situation, especially concerning the large equity loan on our house back home. The Lord replied with His own question: *"Why are you so worried? Look at the whole picture."* That word was followed by a vision of a stairway, with a light shining at its top--a clear allusion to Jacob's dream in Genesis 28. There, in verses 12 and 13, Jacob, while on his way to Bethel, sees a ladder reaching from earth to heaven, with angels ascending and descending on it, and with the Lord himself standing at its top. In biblical imagery, the ladder *was* the Lord, providentially mediating His loving care to mankind below. It seemed that the Lord intended Al's vision as a visual reminder to us of His sovereign care for *us* personally. And if that was, in fact, *the whole picture*, then why, indeed, were we so worried? But consistent trust in that care was obviously not our strong suit, and, to prove the point, I proceeded to ask about selling our house, and questioning if we were ever going back there. At that point, the Lord fired back, *"Who's in charge here?"* But the question only led Allen to lament that we had never understood what we were supposed to be doing, had never been financially successful, and were afraid that we would never be able to find the right thing to do in life! The Lord's next response was a reference to Luke 12:8-20, the Parable of the Rich Fool. There Jesus gives a stern warning about storing up *things*. At the end of it all, Allen finally arrived at what was slowly becoming the pertinent question: "Lord, are we here for me to pursue the priesthood?" A short while later he had a vision of several rows of desks. The front two rows were old-fashioned, while the third was of a different type. Allen came in and sat behind the third desk. We saw this as corroborating that we were to remain in seminary for the full three years, as part of the ordination process.

As the prime provider, Allen's immediate fears were naturally more financially focused, but the Lord's admonition to him had been to look at the *whole* picture. That picture, not by coincidence, was also giving him a wider ministerial perspective. As he later wrote, "Trying to pay bills without money is not fun, but perhaps it's giving me empathy for others who are in the same situation." It seems to be a general rule that when God is doing a work in us, He has both His and our work with *others* in mind. Nothing is ever just about us, or even simply about our current situation.

In light of those principles, I would add that the seminary was offering a 10-day trip to Israel after Christmas, and generous donors were offering financial and child care assistance for those students and their spouses who wanted to go. Their benevolence was confirmed with the Lord's words *"sustain,"* and *"Philadelphia."* Without that "brotherly love," we could not have considered going, but now, as we began to pray about it, the Lord advised, *"Take advantage of the opportunities, and don't worry."* Once more we were reminded that, if the Lord is in something, He will make the way for it to happen. To make the matter even more interesting, the verse He also gave was John 2:4. Here we read that there was a wedding at Cana, in *Galilee,* and Mary informs her Son that the wine has run out. There is an event, but there is also a lack, a need. "Dear woman, why do you involve me? Jesus replied. My time has not yet come."(NIV) Yet next, at Mary's request, He miraculously turns six large stone jars filled with water into excellent wine. He takes advantage of the opportunity to work a miracle, and the guests receive the blessing. We accepted the financial help, and we, too, would go to Galilee. And there, *our* jars would be filled to the brim, the overflow from which would bless many others for years to come.

Meanwhile, however, my own inner battles with fear, insecurity, and self-blame continued. On November 8th, as I asked the Lord for the joy that I was supposed to be seeking, Allen heard Him say, *"Let go!"* But we immediately proceeded to go on to fret, all in one breath, over the state of the world and our own path. Allen was next given an image of a large, slender arch, suggesting grace and a way through, and he heard, *"Do you think it's not under My control?"* It was a rhetorical question. Last, when I asked how I was to *"let go"*, the Lord offered, *"Don't let your history control you. Follow Me!"*

Despite that word, November 23rd found us praying yet again about our house back home, and this time, the Lord replied, *"The question you must answer is, do you want to go back there?"* It was a helpful exercise, for two thoughts came to mind. First, going back would have left us right where we had started, not only literally, but emotionally, spiritually, and vocationally, as well, and for no worthwhile purpose. It was abundantly clear that God had called us out of that situation and even imagining going back made us answer, "No!" But second, the implication was that He would have allowed us to go back if we had made that choice. God respects our free will even when He knows that some choices would be far less than in our own best interest. Indeed, when I next asked about finding what the Lord would have me do, He simply offered the corresponding mental exercise: *"Look how much your life is changed."*

Our lives *were* changed, and changing, but when we further inquired about matters of provision, and why nothing was happening in that regard, the Lord answered, *"I could make it happen, but you need to change."* Now the emphasis was on *us.* That word was accompanied by Isaiah 23, a prophecy concerning the wealthy trade city of Tyre, and the study questions in our bible asked what losses we would find most disastrous: home? business? job? our personal skills? And to what had we looked to fill the void that only God can fill? Once more, the scripture and the questions were too apropos to be a coincidence. In the image that followed, Allen saw a control lever that had to be both pulled out and turned, in order to remain in an "on" position, suggesting that the responsibility to connect with God's power, and stay connected to it, lay with us. When we later asked *how* we needed to change, the Lord gave two hard words in the form of two Biblical characters: *"Absalom,"* and *"Sapphira."* Clearly, pride and issues related to money and security continued to be serious matters that needed to be addressed. It was about our hearts, and not our circumstances. Paul's words from Romans 8:18-21 followed: "I consider that our present sufferings are not worth comparing with the glory that will be revealed in us. The creation waits in eager expectation for the sons of God to be revealed. For the creation was subjected to frustration, not by its own choice, but by the will of the one who subjected it, in hope that the creation itself will be liberated from its bondage to decay and brought into the glorious freedom of the children of God."(NIV) And so, it seems our frustration had a divine source, as well as cosmic implications!

Thankfully, the Lord also affirmed that we were making progress, and He went on to exhort us to draw nearer to Him, through constant prayer. When I asked once more about doing something with the house then or waiting, He replied, *"It doesn't make any difference."* This scripture from the glorious vision recounted by the apostle John in Revelation 7:9, followed: "After this I looked and there before me was a great multitude that no one could count, from every nation, tribe, people, and language, standing before the throne in front of the Lamb. They were wearing white robes and holding palm branches in their hands."(NIV) Talk about our ridiculous worries versus God's sublime finale!

Our semester, as noted, would culminate in our Israel trip, and we next prayed that it would help us to understand our ministry more clearly. The Lord's response, however, seemed to be both more generally directed and more immediately pertinent: *"Make a joyful noise,"* He advised. In the midst of our worries, stress, and frustrations, we needed to be reminded that joy is, after all, our faith's best witness.

December 28th found Allen writing, "I know why Paul said, 'For what I do is not the good I want to do; no, the evil I do not want to do--this I keep on doing.'" (Romans 7:19, NIV) The Lord's gentle reply was, *"There is a Redeemer for the whole world,"* followed by, *"There is much to be done."* The Lord knows our faults and failings, but He graciously sends us on mission, anyway. After all, humanly speaking, we're all He's got, and so He allows our feeble efforts to bless us, bless others, and bless Him.

Speaking of blessing others, on New Years' Day, as Allen awoke, he began to intercede for those who needed to come to the Lord, as well as about the coming Judgment. He heard, *"You've got to warn them, you know."* When Allen asked how, if they're not ready, the Lord said, *"I am preparing their hearts."*

January 5th would find us listening to a lecture in the amphitheater at Caesarea, the port from which St. Paul would depart on his missionary journeys, and later, for Rome, to be martyred. Earlier that morning, as we sat by another sea, the Sea of Galilee, Allen had asked the Lord about our being there, and He had offered, *"There is a purpose in being here in Israel,"* and then, *"You will be my witnesses."*

Speaking of Israel, and of being witnesses, we have already addressed the principle that our lessons are never just for ourselves. In that light, I will add here that, for a variety of reasons, including emotional ones, roughly a year had passed before I was able to write about my major surgery and its surrounding issues, though I had very much wanted to be faithful in the telling of that experience. Finally, I was prodded by an intriguing word from the Lord: *"Terebinth qaneh."* These Hebrew words sent me to the seminary library, where the *terebinth*, I learned, is a solitary tree that grows on the slopes of the mountains of Israel. Also called the turpentine tree, it releases a fragrant resin when the trunk or branches are cut. This resin was a highly valued substance, being sold along the trade routes as a base for both fragrance and turpentine. *"Qaneh"* is the Hebrew word for both *trunk* and *branch*. Thus, I saw that I had been called to be a terebinth tree which, having been cut, both literally and figuratively, would release a fragrant fluid, through spoken and written testimony which would hopefully bless and help to heal others. Of course, it goes without saying that my situation in that regard will eternally pale in comparison with the story of Christ, the Righteous Branch, who was cut and who shed His fragrant Blood for us, and for our salvation. But we can imitate Him, and He credits that as enough.

In summation, our time in Ambridge had indeed begun as a change of locus and a change of focus. It was a place for training and a time to heal. As the Lord's plans began to flesh out and unfold, that year would turn into four, as we gradually discerned a call to ordination to the priesthood. It would be a time of trust and anxiety, of fear and yet a high sense of adventure, of hope and confusion, of joy and struggle, of choices, decisions, and demands. It was to be an intense and richly blessed time of learning, stretching, growing, confirmation of call, healing, and academic and professional preparation for full-time ministry, all in the context of a vibrant seminary community. That process, in turn, would lead us on to a parish in Mentone, Alabama, a later transfer of ordination to the Anglican Communion, and several years of home church. But there was yet more to come on our "most excellent adventure."

In that light, I must first pause to state that not everyone is called to seminary or to ordination. In His rich economy, the Lord has a dazzling variety of callings and vocations for His children. Our calling was simply His path for us, and even that path would continue to take some astonishing and unexpected turns. Ultimately, our "yet more to come" would, among other things, lead us to Christ's One, Holy, Catholic and

Apostolic Church. Indeed, in going over our journals from even this very early time, we can now see many, many hints of that, embedded, in various forms, in the abundant scriptures, words, and visions we received. Looking back, we have discovered that these intimations were *everywhere*, tucked away, like little jewels, and waiting to be discovered. Thus, we feel we would be remiss if we did not conclude by relating two fascinating incidences of God's work of hearing, healing, and purpose, from a Catholic perspective.

The first incident was related to us by a cousin of mine who was working for a military contractor. It seems that the bladder on a fuel tank was being repaired, and the fellow working on it, who was not wearing an oxygen mask at the time, due to the tightness of the space, was overcome by the toxic fumes, and had turned blue. My cousin John called his wife to ask for advice, and she said, "Put a brown scapular on him," to which he replied, "I don't have one." She insisted, "Give him *yours*." John did so, but when the fellow was placed in the ambulance, John believed from the man's appearance that he was already dead. John went to the hospital the next morning, fully expecting to hear that the man had died, but, to his astonishment, he found the fellow sitting up in a chair, dressed and completely well! He was discharged the next day. Amazingly, the doctor there told John that when the man had arrived at the hospital, he had evidenced no brain activity whatsoever! (I should explain that the brown scapular is a Marian sacramental given to St. Simon Stock by the Blessed Virgin Mary, under her title of Our Lady of Mount Carmel, in an apparition in England back in the early Middle Ages. Made of thin pieces of brown wool and worn over the shoulders, it has been the source of numerous instances of healing as well as other miracles over the centuries. I would add that the scapular has no power of its own. Rather, God's power is released through prayer, discipline, and faith. The Lord often uses things of the material world to work miracles, through the power of His Spirit).

In the second incident, some years ago my father lay dying from a combination of kidney and congestive heart failure. The medications worked at cross-purposes, and we knew that the end was near. For three weeks, I spent a good part of each day standing over his bed in the nursing home as I tried to coax some fluids into him and soothe his distress. It was a hot May day in Alabama, and my attention to my father caused me to neglect my own need for fluids. That, in combination with fatigue, stress, grief, and the physical posture of leaning over his bed for hours at a time eventually resulted in the development of a bladder and kidney infection. However, so focused was I on my father that I was oblivious to my own condition.

At length my father passed away, but, shortly afterwards, I was alerted to my own situation when a visit to the bathroom resulted in copious blood pouring from my bladder. Before the prescribed anti-biotics could take effect, I had a miserable fever and painfully infected kidneys. A few days later, as I sat by myself in prayer, I was led to open my eyes and look down at my hands, which were resting palm up in my lap. To my astonishment, I had a vision in which I seemed to be holding, from left to right, blood, ashes, and water. As I pondered this, I recalled the passage from Numbers 19 that described the procedure required after contact with the dead and dying. In this ritual, an unblemished red heifer was slaughtered outside the camp, and its *blood* sprinkled by the priest. The heifer was then *burned*, along with cedar wood, hyssop, and scarlet wool, after which the priest was required to wash both his body and his clothes with *water*, and to remain ceremonially unclean until evening. Next, a man free from defilement was to take some of the heifer's ashes, mix them with running water, and then, dipping a bunch of hyssop into the pot, was to sprinkle the contaminated person on the third and seventh day. Finally, the "unclean" person was to make atonement, and he, as well as the "clean" person, were required to wash their garments and bathe themselves in water, on the evening of which they both became clean again. Both the Israelites and the aliens living among them were to keep this as a lasting ordinance.

First, why were the Israelites required to perform this elaborate ritual? And why was the Lord showing me these things in relation to my own situation? After all, aren't we people of the New Covenant? And hasn't the old order passed away? So what did these things have to do with my health, my healing, my shalom? I was intrigued to note that, looking left to right, what I had experienced first was cleansing by means of the *blood* that had poured out of me. That image was followed by the fever, and an unrelenting sensation of burning in my back: the *fire*. And last, I was prompted to drink lots of *water* to re-hydrate my body and flush out my system. While suffering from the hot pain and fever, I prayed about the amazing imagery, and the Lord showed me that my vision was even more specific, and vastly more profound, than I would have imagined. He said: "It's about purification. There is not just one way that you are cleansed, though all ways work together. My blood is the ultimate cleansing, but the water and the fire also cleanse. The ashes are an image of cleansing by fire, and that often does bring the most pain. It is happening now; that is why the ashes were in the center."

We indeed note from scripture that the ashes were at the center. They were the focus, as it were, for it was these that were later to be used in the ritual of the water of cleansing, whose purpose was the purification from sin, and they were to be kept for use for others who would come into contact with the dead. But here, I now saw other themes, other motifs, as well. There was the contrast made in Hebrews 9 between the blood of the red heifer, sprinkled for outward cleanliness, and Christ's blood, shed for our redemption. Then there was the fire of judgment, as well as the fire of the outpouring of the Holy Spirit at Pentecost. Last, there were the waters of repentance, reconciliation, and baptism--*all of this* connected through the concepts of death, holiness, healing, and God's eternal purposes. My infection was healed, but, years later, I continue to ponder the unfathomable richness of the three-part image and its implications and applications. The sacramental life of the Catholic Church had been on abundant display in my vision, years before I had even become Catholic. What's more, I had been treated to a unique and profound personal window into the Church's teaching that the New Covenant is concealed in the Old, and the Old is revealed in the New.

Among other things, what intrigues me here is that, although we are no longer required to follow the old cultic laws of ritual observance, the eternal archetypes behind them are apparently as real and meaningful as ever in the mind of God. The ritual cleansing was a reminder to the Israelites, and no doubt to me as well, that physical disease, death, and bodily corruption are the result of sin, and that contact with the dead and dying rendered even the persons who touched them and who assisted in the ritual, unclean.

Lest we think that the idea of uncleanness is utterly irrelevant to us today, let us remember that the concept stemmed from the dilemma of a holy God confronted with a fallen and corrupt world. Does this mean that we are to return to the *old cultic rituals*? Obviously not, for Paul called the Galatians who thought so, bewitched. But here is the point. Though the Old Covenant *rituals* are no longer required, the moral and spiritual templates remain as eternal truths, superceded and assisted by new and more powerful rites, and God's goal for us remains shalom.

In closing, I offer the following from my recent Lenten session in the confessional. It had been an especially difficult Lent for me, as I had, for some reason, found myself to be repeatedly recalling and struggling with my history of sporadic mental and physical abuse from my beloved parents. I was puzzled at my reactions, as well as miserable in my concern over my spiritual and emotional state. Here is the pastoral advice offered by our priest. First, "a Lent is given to each of us, and the Lord's medicine is different for each." Suddenly, I realized that it was the Lord Himself who had initiated my experience in order to allow for new healing. It was His personally targeted Lenten gift to me. Next, the priest counseled:

"Forgive your parents"

"Keep giving God your time."

"Persevere." And, most interestingly,

"Embrace the poverty of the situation."

I took the latter to mean that I was to accept my helplessness in the situation and my need for God's help. I pass these on as God's wisdom given through our priest, as well as excellent general advice.

"Come, Holy Spirit. We invite You into the very depths of our being. Lead us, guide us, coach us, encourage and challenge us. Direct us in all things. Teach us to become great decision makers, so that in every moment of every day, we can choose what is right, noble and just. Amen."

9

⤛⤜

Some Final Points to Review and to Ponder

There is a dynamic that can be seen throughout our narratives, as summarized here:

1) God has a specific plan and purpose for each life.

2) God is present and at work all the time, whether we see it, know it, or even, perhaps, agree with it. He is a God of surprises, and He is in charge.

3) God is a jealous God, by self-definition, and He will do whatever it takes, from His end, to bring us to recognition and fulfillment of His purposes for us. The corollary is that we must be listening. What we see as awful may bring the greatest blessing.

4) We can only hear what we can hear at the moment. There is no other way. God uses it all, but our path usually follows a zigzag trajectory.

5) Ease is not part of God's plan. Roadblocks are often *God's* obstacles, used as a test and a confirmation that He is at work. Blessings come from difficulties, not ease.

6) God takes us where we are, but He doesn't want to leave us there, and He doesn't force us.

7) We are never simply healed *from* something. We are always healed *for* something. God's goal is that His purposes become our purposes. That is the meaning of salvation.

8) God works both by creating trust and by instilling a holy fear--an interesting conundrum.

9) Part of our healing process is learning to discern the cause of our pain. Is it from God or us, and how do we determine the difference?

10) Since we have free will, if we insist, God will ultimately leave us to our own devices.

11) Divine providence informs us that everything happens for a reason.

12) We are called to embrace the joy of uncertainty. Like Abraham, we can't know the details of our journey before we start.

13) Given our free will, and the dynamic relationship between cause and effect, we will always be in a spiritual battle to find and keep shalom. But it is that very struggle, that holy *discomfort*, that stretching of the spiritual muscles, that gives ultimate joy, and a real and lively relationship with God and others.

14) We have been given both freedom *from* and freedom *for*. God takes risks, and He knows the outcome, if we obey, and the consequences, if we disobey.

15) We can't move toward our destiny, our purpose in God, if we choose to be locked in the prison of our past.

16) Doing and being are corollaries. One is the natural consequence of the other.

17) It is sometimes OK, and even necessary, to get away from destructive people and circumstances. Granted, this is not always possible, in which case the test is always our response in the midst of the situation.

18) When does God's call in our life have its beginning? Typically, long before we begin to realize it has.

19) Our necessary *movement* in life always begins with the spiritual, but it may also be physical, and it almost always involves hard work. There is no retirement in the spiritual life.

20 Not all of our *movement* is of God, but He can still use it, correct it, or redirect it. Meanwhile, He can still use us where we are.

21) We have learned far more from, and been far more blessed by, the sufferings and the challenges, than from ease.

22) In the human arena, all is the result of God's response to the things that we do, or fail to do.

23) There is a difference between pausing for guidance and stagnation.

24) Your story, your pain is a part of who you are. Either you will cooperate with God and He will use it to His glory, as well as for your blessing and that of many others, or Satan will use it to your destruction and the grief of those who love you and care about you.